Chief Joseph (1832-1904)
"We are all children of one mother, so why should we quarrel?" Photo courtesy The Smithsonian Institution National Anthropological Archives. Negative 2906.

LEGENDS OF THE GREAT CHIEFS

by

Emerson N. Matson

STORYPOLE PRESS

Tacoma

All rights reserved under International and Pan-American
Conventions. Published in Tacoma, Washington by The
Storypole Press, 11015 Bingham Avenue East, Tacoma,
Washington 98446.

Second edition April 1984

Cover photo courtesy of Smithsonian Institution. Permission is
gratefully acknowledged.

Library of Congress Cataloging in Publication Data

Matson, Emerson N   comp.
    Legends of the great chiefs.

    CONTENTS: Nisqually legends as remembered by P.
Leschi: Cougar, Wildcat, and the giant; Blue Jay and the moon
legend; Coyote and the witches.—Oglala Sioux Legends, recalled
from the days of Chief Red Cloud: Legend of the peace pipe;
Legend of the Wind Cave; Legend of Crazy Horse. [etc.]
    1. Indians of North America—Legends. [1. Indians of North
America—Legends] I. Title.
E98.F6M32   398.2'09701   72–5870
ISBN 0–9609940–0–9

Also by Emerson N. Matson

LONGHOUSE LEGENDS

*Dedicated to
my wife, Jo Anne,
and her mother, Ellen Porter,
for their inspiration, encouragement, and help.*

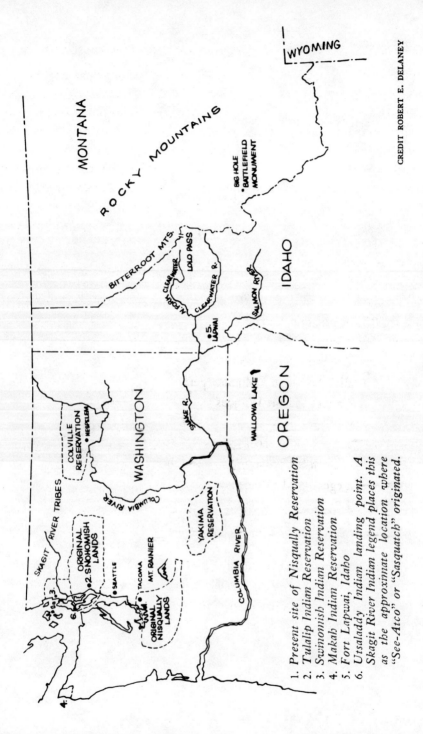

CREDIT ROBERT E. DELANEY

1. Present site of Nisqually Reservation
2. Tulalip Indian Reservation
3. Swinomish Indian Reservation
4. Makah Indian Reservation
5. Fort Lapwai, Idaho
6. Utsaladdy Indian landing point. A Skagit River Indian legend places this as the approximate location where "See-Atco" or "Sasquatch" originated.

Contents

Legends of the Great Chiefs

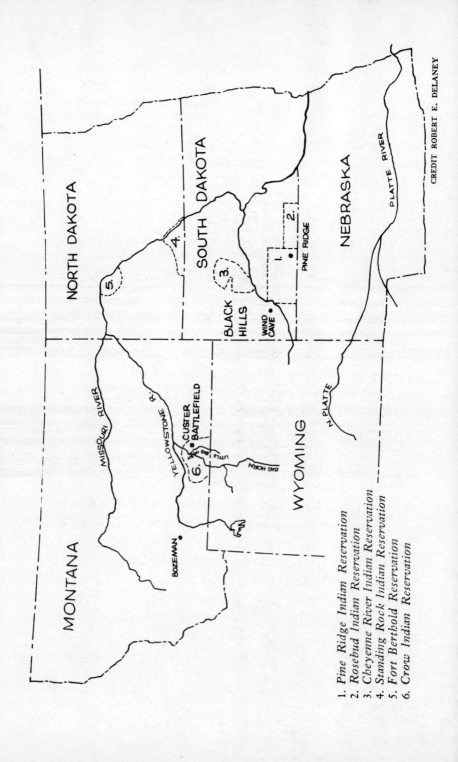

1. Pine Ridge Indian Reservation
2. Rosebud Indian Reservation
3. Cheyenne River Indian Reservation
4. Standing Rock Indian Reservation
5. Fort Berthold Reservation
6. Crow Indian Reservation

CREDIT ROBERT E. DELANEY

Preface

From the pounding surf along the Pacific Ocean beaches to the restless, windswept grasslands of the western Plains, the culture of the American Indian was maintained by the telling and retelling of tribal and family legends.

Whether the legends originated with a Makah fisherman living on the westernmost tip of the United States mainland or a Sioux hunter camped on the Dakota plains, they usually conveyed a common command that was accepted as law. Cleanliness of mind, word, and body was the basic lesson. The everyday routines of the Indians were affected by these old stories. This was especially true in the case of tribal leaders.

Chief Red Cloud, the famous Sioux general and diplomat, arose early each morning to bathe in cold water. He would follow his bath with a prayer using the peace pipe. Sitting Bull was known to take daily baths, and to offer morning and evening prayers with his peace pipe. The same practice was a daily ritual westward across the plains of the Dakotas, Montana, Wyoming, Idaho, to Washington and Oregon. Chief Swan took daily salt- and freshwater baths to cleanse his body before praying beside a sacred rock near Neah Bay, Washington. The coastal and Puget Sound Indians did not use a peace pipe, but instead prayed in a special, sacred place.

There was a thread of similarity woven into all Indian legends that told of man's creation. These stories featured a trickster, who through magic and special powers, traveled the land to prepare the world for the coming of modern man. The Indians believed that at one time all creatures spoke a common language, and lived as one tribe. Knowing that mankind would not be happy with this arrangement, the changer made the world into a place to support man.

The changer took a different identity in each section of the country. For the Plains Indian, he appeared as Iktomi, the spider. Nez Percé, Yakimas, Nisqually and most Puget Sound tribes saw him as Spealhyi, the coyote. Out on the Washington coast the changer was known as Kwatee. Changer stories recorded in this book include "Coyote and the Witches" (Nisqually), "Iktomi and the Ducks" (Sioux), "Coyote and the Monster" (Nez Percé), "Legend of Kwatee" (Makah), and "Raven and Pheasant" (Skagit).

Some legends were used as reminders for children to observe the rules and overcome the problems caused by community social living. These stories in various forms were common among the Puget Sound and coastal tribes where many families lived in one house. The Snohomish legend of Sway-Uock is an example. It was used to make certain that early evening bedtime was a time of peace and quiet.

Coastal families lived under the constant threat of enemy raids. The raiders would invade from the sea and often carry off youngsters as slaves. The Makah legend of Ishcus was told to keep children from wandering off without supervision.

The completed text of this book represents nearly three years of research and gathering material. I made numerous visits to reservations, and talked to many Indian people, and as they traced their family trees for me, it became increasingly clear that they have a deep-felt concern for the future of the legends.

A number of the Indian elders expressed regret that many younger Indians have turned their backs on the old culture in favor of the materialistic ways of the white man. And a few were quick to point out the evils that have plagued their race since the first white trader arrived with whiskey, gunpowder, and disease.

For some tribes, many of the tribal songs and legends have long been interred in burial grounds with the people who once sang or told them. The surviving members who now crave a link with their past can no longer find a trace of their tribal culture. This book is an effort to preserve a few of the old legends and the history of those who told them.

The legends, when told in the tribal language, seem to be more entertaining than when translated into English. "In our own language, we can make ourselves be more a part of the story," one elderly man explained. "We who know the legends first heard them in our own language." Some storytellers partially dramatized the stories by using

the hands to show antlers, large ears, or a large nose. This
seemed to add considerable amusement for both teller and
listener.

In addition to personal interview, information came from
pioneers' diaries, museums, old manuscripts, and previously
published material. Many people were helpful with re-
search and deserve recognition for their contributions.
Grateful thanks go to Father Paul B. Steinmetz, S. J., of
Sacred Heart Mission, Pine Ridge, South Dakota; Harold
E. Johnston, Rapid City, South Dakota; Swinomish Chief
Martin Sampson, my longtime friend; Paul Leschi, a Nis-
qually; Harriet Shelton Dover, a Snohomish; Juanita
Brown, a Yakima; Mrs. Helen Selma Ward, daughter of
Makah Chief Swan; Tall-Kin-Kin-My, great-niece of Nez
Percé Chief Joseph; Frank White Buffalo Man; and Edgar
Red Cloud, both Sioux.

I.

Nisqually Legends

As remembered by Paul Leschi

Paul Leschi was born on the Nisqually Reservation in 1889, and spent most of his life fishing the Nisqually River commercially under the Medicine Creek Treaty agreement.

He remembered the early days of Washington statehood when many of the Indians traveled from homesteader to homesteader shearing sheep for five cents a head. He remembered the rich folklore he inherited when born the great-grandson of Quiemulth and great-grandnephew of Leschi.

These great chiefs led approximately 150 warriors against settlers during the Washington Territorial Indian War of 1855–56. The Nisqually went to war when the territorial government attempted to force them to vacate rich grasslands and move to a reservation on a high forested bluff. The Indians were certain that they and their horses could not survive on the 1,280 acres designated as their reservation.

Following a series of encounters with reinforced troops, most of the braves returned to the reservation. Quiemulth finally decided to turn himself in after receiving promises of fair treatment. The military escorted him to the office of Territorial Governor Isaac Stevens in Olympia.

Fearing for Quiemulth's safety, the governor allowed the Indian to use his office for the night, and assigned a guard to protect him. During the night, Quiemulth was shot while he slept. His murderer was never arrested or brought to trial.

The settlers were anxious to remove any further threat of war or Indian raids, and demanded that Leschi also be brought back to the settlement. Rather than send troops into the mountains to search for the Nisqually chief, the settlers sent a cousin of Leschi to persuade the chief to surrender himself. Carrying a message of peace and guarantees for Leschi's personal safety, the cousin was successful in betraying the Nisqually war chief. As the pair approached Fort Steilacoom, Leschi was seized by the United States Army and thrown into jail.

He was quickly brought to trial for a murder he did not commit and was sentenced to be hanged. On the day of his execution, the hangmen refused to take the life of an innocent man, and the Nisqually warrior was taken to Olympia.

A second trial was held, and once again the court ordered Leschi hanged. The army carried out the execution on the edge of the Nisqually Reservation boundary. Chief Leschi is now buried in an Indian cemetery in Tacoma, Washington.

The land of the Nisqually Indian nation extended from Puget Sound to the east of Mount Rainier in western Washington. Most of the Nisqually villages in the mountainous areas were bilingual. They spoke both the Salish language of Puget Sound Canoe tribes and a Pacific Northwest plains language called Shahaptin.

Nisqually Indians traded freely with the Yakimas, a tribe that inhabited the plains of eastern Washington. From the Yakimas they secured Nez Percé horses and were the only Puget Sound tribe to maintain large herds of these animals.

COUGAR, WILDCAT, AND THE GIANT

At one time Cougar and Wildcat lived together in a cave near the river.

While Cougar would roam the countryside hunting for food, Wildcat would stay near the cave and tend the fire. Wildcat loved to sleep, and sometimes he would doze off, waking just in time to save the last ember.

Cougar knew his cousin had a weakness for falling asleep, so before each hunting trip he would warn Wildcat, "Keep the fire going; do not fall asleep and let it go out."

Wildcat tried to follow his cousin's instructions, but one time when he was sitting beside the fire and watching the flames dance, he was lulled into a deep sleep.

Slowly the fire died and was replaced by a pile of cold ashes. When Wildcat awakened, he tried and tried to re-kindle the flames, but he could not get a fire started.

Across the river a small column of smoke was visible curling up from a clump of trees. Wildcat knew the fire belonged to a giant who often camped there. He also knew how dangerous it would be to try to steal the giant's fire.

Wildcat faced a dilemma. To tell Cougar that the fire had gone out would make his cousin very angry. Cougar might become so angry that he would force Wildcat to leave the cave and find a new home. And then Wildcat would have to do his own hunting, tend his own fire, and have less time to sleep.

After thinking his problem over, Wildcat decided to risk stealing the giant's fire. He swam the river and cautiously crept to the edge of the giant's camp.

The giant was away, and Wildcat acted quickly. He seized the burning sticks and quickly wrapped his long tail around them. As he swam back across the river, he used his tail to hold the sticks high above the water to keep them dry.

By the time Wildcat had reached midstream, the flames had crawled down the sticks and were scorching his tail. Despite the great pain, he managed to keep his tail erect and the flames above the water.

Wildcat was thankful to have made his way back to the cave, but his tail was very sore. He dropped the burning sticks on a pile of dry shavings and had a bigger campfire than ever.

In the early evening Cougar returned, dragging a deer killed during the day. Before Wildcat could explain what had happened, Cougar began sniffing the fire.

"Our campfire smells different this evening, cousin," Cougar commented. Then Wildcat revealed how he had stolen the fire from across the river.

He showed Cougar how the fire had burned his once proud tail to a mere stub. Cougar failed to offer sympathy to the ailing cat, for he was too worried about the giant's reaction. The giant was known to have a violent temper.

"What shall we do when the giant discovers the theft and comes looking for us?" Cougar asked. "He might even eat us."

"We must cook all our meat for him," Wildcat answered. "We'll feed him so much there'll be no room left in his stomach for us."

From across the river they could hear shouts from the enraged giant. "Somebody has stolen my fire, and I'll catch the thief," he growled.

"The giant is about to cross the river. We must start preparing food," Cougar instructed.

Wildcat quickly began to tie the venison to cooking sticks and soon the cousins were roasting the entire deer. They also added grouse, rabbit, and other small game that had been stored in the cave.

Cougar looked out into the evening dusk and saw that the giant was wading the river. "He is huge," Cougar observed. "All the animals of the forest would have to swim where he is wading with ease."

"The smell of my fire will lead me to the ones who left me without flames," the giant proclaimed as he climbed the riverbank and headed for the pair.

The cousins were trembling with fear and decided they must persuade the giant that Wildcat took the fire so that they could hold a feast in his honor.

"We're over here," Cougar called out. "We've been cooking your favorite foods, and we were about to invite you to a special dinner as our honored guest."

"A dinner cooked over fire you took from my shelter," grunted the giant, staring down at the pair. "The brightness of your offer is clouded by your treachery."

"Please eat," Wildcat pleaded. "Eat all you want. You are our honored guest."

"I will eat all I want," the giant replied. "I'll eat all the food you've prepared, and then I might eat you, too."

The giant sat down on a fallen tree and began to eat. He ate and ate, greedily devouring all the meat that had been prepared.

"I don't feel like eating you now," the giant told the cousins, but added, "I'll save you for later." Cougar and Wildcat were ordered to sit by their cave while the giant stretched out on the ground next to the fire.

"I'm going to sleep now, but when I awake, I'll have you for my breakfast," he said with a yawn.

Waiting until they were sure the giant was sound asleep, the Cougar and Wildcat quietly slipped from the camp and ran into the forest. The pair fled deeper and deeper into the heavy timber until they thought they had left the giant far behind. Then they sat down to rest.

Before the two could catch their breath, they heard the giant crashing through an underbrush in pursuit. "Hurry! He's closer than we thought," warned Cougar. And they retreated deeper into the woods.

Cougar and Wildcat ran all night trying to escape the powerful giant. He was a strong runner, and with his great size even the largest windfall was an easy step.

Approaching a stand of cottonwood trees, the cousins decided on a plan. They each picked an armload of cottonwood seeds and hid near the trail.

As the giant came upon them they threw the seeds into his face. The cottonlike clusters filled his mouth and nostrils, and he choked on the fibers. Spitting fluff and coughing, the giant was forced to give up the chase.

Cougar and Wildcat came to a fork in the trail and sat down to decide which way to go. After a lengthy discussion, they could not agree.

"I think we should take the path which leads to the valley," Wildcat insisted. "In the valley we'll be close to water, small game, and shelter from the wind."

"The upper path leads to the high meadows filled with feeding deer and elk," argued Cougar. "My favorites are fawns and elk calves."

The cousins each became more stubborn, and finally Cougar suggested they end their long friendship and separate.

"That suits me fine," snarled Wildcat. "I'm a good hunter and never needed your help anyway."

"Wildcat can't keep a fire so I don't know what makes him think he can hunt," Cougar thought as he headed up the high trail.

Many weeks passed, and the warm summer days gave way to snowflakes and icy winds. Cougar followed the deer herds down the mountain to areas where browsing was more plentiful.

He had not felt the warmth of a fire since leaving Wildcat, and he was cold. He often longed for Wildcat's company, but was too proud to return to the valley and search for him.

Early one morning Cougar was dragging a freshly killed deer to his shelter when he heard a noise in the ravine below. Looking over the bank he saw a very skinny Wildcat picking the remains of a freshly cooked rabbit.

"Hello, down there," called Cougar. "May I come to your dinner?"

"Is that you, cousin?" answered Wildcat, who was very surprised. "Please come down and join me, but all I've got is a small rabbit."

Accepting the invitation, Cougar climbed down to Wildcat, bringing his fresh kill as a surprise. Seeing the deer, Wildcat confessed that the small rabbit was the first food he had eaten in weeks.

Cougar invited his hungry cousin to roast the venison while he warmed up by the fire. "This is the first time I've warmed myself over a fire since we lived at the cave," Cougar admitted.

The pair agreed that they did better together. Working as a team, they were able to escape the angry giant. Together they always had food and warmth. And they were never lonely.

"I've learned one thing since we took separate trails," Cougar volunteered. "When you have a close friend, you should look for his good points rather than his faults."

"And two can accomplish much more than one," Wildcat added.

BLUE JAY AND THE MOON LEGEND

Long before the great mountains were there, and even before the first snowflake fell, the Great Spirit assigned the moon to light the world during the hours of darkness.

Every night as darkness began to blanket the land, the moon would rise into the heavens and provide the people with light. When daylight began to break, the moon would retire until darkness came again.

One night, the people of the world looked into the dark sky. Only the stars could be seen, for the moon was not there. They thought the moon had forgotten to wake up for his night's work.

"Who will wake up the moon?" the great chief asked

the people and all the creatures of the world. But no one answered until the beautiful blue jay volunteered.

"I am indeed a clever bird," the haughty jay told the people. "I'll fly to the edge of the world and wake up the moon."

"If you're going to awaken the moon, Blue Jay, then let me give you some advice on how to pass through the end-of-the-world door," the great chief advised.

"I don't have time to listen," Blue Jay replied. "I must leave immediately, as the hour is late and the journey is far."

Before the great chief could instruct Blue Jay, the bird was sailing through the evergreens in its search for the end of the world. In the darkness, Blue Jay landed near the top of a tall cedar tree. Hopping from limb to limb to the very top, he then sailed to an even taller tree.

As the jay was hopping to the top of the next tree, he met an owl. "Who is there?" called Owl through the darkness.

"It's me, Blue Jay," the bird answered. "I'm going to the end of the world to awaken the moon. We fear he has overslept, and we need his light."

"When you get to the end of the world, you will find a door that's opening and closing," said Owl.

"I know, I know," interrupted Blue Jay. "I'll figure it out when I get there. Now I must leave, for the hour is late and the journey far." And he hopped to a higher branch before spreading his wings and flying to a still taller tree.

The jay was exhausted when he arrived at the end of the world. He had climbed the world's tallest trees in order to reach his destination.

As the owl had warned, there was a door that kept opening and closing. When the door opened, Blue Jay could see the moon seated on the edge of his bed whittling on a stick.

The door opened and shut, never pausing long enough to allow Blue Jay to pass through. Finally, after watching the door open and shut many times, the jay thought he had figured out the timing, and he flew at the opening. But when he arrived, the big door slammed shut.

The poor jay had flown into the heavy door with such force it had flattened his forehead and made a bump on the top of his head. He jumped around in great pain, and as the door opened again, he accidentally hopped through and into the bedroom of the moon.

"Katchi, Katchi," was all Blue Jay could say to the startled moon, for the pain from the blow on his head was still great.

"Who gave you the authority to pass through the door into my bedroom?" Moon demanded. "Why did you not heed the advice offered during your journey? It would have saved you much pain."

Still suffering, the jay found words to explain that the sun had set in the west, and the world was very dark.

"All living creatures of the world thought you had overslept, and I came to awaken you," Blue Jay said. "I was in a hurry and did not have time to stop and listen to advice," the bird admitted.

"So it is with many people," Moon stated. "Many times, to stop and listen to sound advice would save much pain later."

Then Moon looked at the jay's flattened forehead and the huge bump on top of his head.

"Feathers will soon grow over the bump on your head, making a crest," Moon said. "Your crest will serve to warn all living creatures that, when advice is offered, time should be taken to listen to it."

Blue Jay protested, "You're being unfair. Had you awakened on time, I wouldn't have had to make the trip through the darkness." The bird shouted at the moon, "This is your fault, not mine."

"You speak with a loud and disrespectful tongue," Moon said. "The people must be reminded that, if they ever send a person to the end of the world again, he must speak with respect. You will carry that reminder. Your voice will continue to be loud and coarse, but the only word you will be able to say is 'Katchi.' "

"Haw, haw," scoffed Blue Jay. "Because you're too lazy to get up on time, you talk of punishment."

The moon explained that the Great Spirit had spoken and had ordered him not to shine until later that night. "For making false accusations, you deserve to lose your tongue," the moon charged. "You're lucky you've been spared so that you can say 'Katchi.' "

The jay watched the moon whittle a point on the end of his stick. When he had finished, he handed the stick to Blue Jay, telling him to use the stick to prop against the swinging door when he left.

"This is the advice your chief tried to give you, as did the owl," Moon stated. "Had you heeded it, you would have passed through the door without injury."

The moon then promised to light the world for the balance of the night so that the jay would be able to find his way home.

This legend was an important part of the training of

young Nisqually. Blue jays were common to the area, and inhabited the brush surrounding Nisqually villages. Every time the jays would scream, "Katchi, Katchi," the children were reminded to listen to advice and to speak with respect.

COYOTE AND THE WITCHES

Every year salmon would swarm into the Nisqually River and migrate upstream to spawn.

The Indians looked forward to this fish run, because salmon were an important source of their food supply. So when the first fish of a run were sighted, it was reason for celebration.

One year the Nisqually Indians living along the upper river waited and waited for salmon. The waters flowing by their villages were without fish, and this worried the chief.

He sent a scout downstream to find out if salmon had entered the river. Walking along the riverbank, the scout often stopped and waded out into the clear water. But he couldn't find a trace of salmon.

Many miles downstream he came to the camp of five squaws, who were said to be evil witches. Their camp was full of freshly smoked salmon.

The scout found a large dam and a fish trap just below the squaws' camp. The dam was constructed so that it completely blocked the salmon from migrating upstream.

Undetected by the witches, the scout slipped back into the dense forest and hurried home to announce his discovery to his people.

Hearing that the witches were responsible for the lack of salmon, the chief and the village leaders held a great powwow.

"If we send warriors to attack their village, the witches will cast an evil spell on us," the chief told the village leaders. "Such a course could bring sickness and death to our families," he said. "We must find a way to open their dam without alarming them."

Listening to the chief's plea, Coyote stepped forward. "I have a plan that will fill the river with salmon," he told the council.

The coyote, whose name was Spealyhi, built a baby's basket. Carefully sealing the lower part of the basket to make it watertight, he climbed in and covered himself with a goat-hair blanket. Then he asked the Indians to push him into the current of the river.

The river carried him through the rapids, around the great rocks, and soon he had drifted into the squaws' fish-trap dam.

Spealyhi's basket was discovered a short time later by the eldest of the squaws. She pulled him from the water and up onto a rocky bank. Without looking into the basket, she ran to tell the others of her find.

"I found a baby's basket drifting in the river," she told her sister witches. "We must go back and care for the child. We'll raise him to be our slave."

"First we must dig camas roots," the others decided. "There'll be plenty of time to take care of the child when our work is done." The five squaws headed for the prairie in search of camas.

When Spealyhi was sure the witches had left, he climbed

from his basket and went to the dam. Carefully removing some of the center poles, he allowed many salmon to escape upstream. At about the time he thought the squaws would return, the coyote skillfully replaced the poles and crept back to his basket.

The witches did not return from digging camas roots until the sun began to set in the west. By the time the squaws returned to check on the child, darkness had covered the forest, and they could not see that he was a coyote.

Each night a different sister would leave a piece of smoked salmon in Spealyhi's basket for him to eat the next day.

Every day, while the squaws were away, Spealyhi would open the dam. And each day he would leave it open a little longer.

The squaws noted that they were catching fewer and fewer fish. "Somebody has been emptying our trap," they agreed. "We must catch this person and punish him."

One day one of the witches accidentally broke her root digger. Since day was nearing an end, the squaws decided to return to their shelter early.

Spealyhi was still on the trap when the squaws reached their camp. "It appears that your abandoned child has turned into a fish-stealing coyote," the four younger witches said to their older sister. "Your kindness has cost us many salmon and permitted the upper-river people to catch our fish."

"You are as guilty as I," the eldest countered. "Was it not you who took turns leaving a piece of salmon each night?"

"But it was you who told us this thief was a harmless child," they answered. "You must pay a penalty as well as the coyote."

While the witches were arguing his fate, Spealyhi pulled the remaining poles from the riverbed, destroying the fish trap and allowing the upper river to fill with countless silvery salmon.

His act went unnoticed, as the witches became angrier and angrier. Finally the four younger squaws tried to cast an evil spell on their powerful older sister. The eldest, who was as evil as her four sisters combined, retaliated. Both sides turned each other into caddis flies.

Spealyhi returned to the village and told the people how he had destroyed the witches' dam, and what fate had befallen the witches.

A great celebration was held, and the coyote was honored for his bravery. All upper-river Indians attended.

During the celebration the great chief proclaimed, "Now generations to come will be able to catch salmon in these waters, no matter where they live. And the salmon will be free to everyone."

II.

Oglala Sioux Legends

Recalled from the days of Chief Red Cloud

The role of the Sioux in western Plains history is a legend in itself. From Fort Reno to Fort Laramie, from the Little Bighorn to Wounded Knee, many distinguished chiefs emerged from the ranks of the Oglala Sioux.

The great Sioux chiefs were famous for their display of generalship and courage on the field of battle. But few achieved greater historical prominence in both war and peace than Chief Red Cloud. During the latter half of the nineteenth century, the history of the northern Plains revolved around him.

Recognition as a warrior and key Sioux leader came to Red Cloud following a series of battles with American troops along the Bozeman Trail, a shortcut to the Montana gold fields. Until 1867, the government had ignored Red Cloud, regarding him as a troublemaker with only a few followers. Then he ambushed and wiped out the eighty-one-man command of Captain William J. Fetterman and had to be taken seriously.

Sioux forces dominated the areas surrounding Fort Kearny and Fort Smith, in the Montana-Wyoming-Dakota region. Because of this display of power, the government had to make peace with Red Cloud on his own terms. These terms included the abandonment and burning of three army posts in Sioux Powder River country. It also gave the Sioux large land holdings designated as the Great Sioux Reservation.

As settlers and prospectors began to move in on unceded Sioux territory, the Indians once again prepared for war. The government invited Red Cloud to Washington, D.C., hoping he would be overwhelmed by the sight of the East's large cities. Instead he became more forceful in pressing his demands.

The Sioux chief's strong position inspired influential admirers, and he was invited to speak at the Cooper Institute in New York City. His words impressed both the overflow crowd and members of the press. Eastern support for Red Cloud became evident, and the government was forced to grant his requests.

Red Cloud's diplomatic victories were nullified when the Sioux agency was removed from the Platte River in 1873. One year later, Colonel George A. Custer violated the Treaty of 1868 by making an expedition into the Black Hills to confirm rumors of gold. His reports of "gold-bearing quartz out of every hill" unleashed droves of prospectors flocking into the Sioux's most sacred country.

A government offer to purchase the treasured Black Hills from the Indians was rejected by Red Cloud. The government was then faced with the dilemma of either evicting its own citizens who invaded Sioux land or employing military force to bring the Indians to terms. A military solution was planned.

The government directed all nontreaty Sioux to report

in to agencies or be subject to attack by the army. This caused great concern among the young men of the agency, and many, including Red Cloud's son Jack, rallied to the support of hostile leaders Crazy Horse and Sitting Bull.

Jack Red Cloud rode with the hostiles when they defeated General Crook at the Rosebud River, June 7, 1876, and a few days later fought in the greatest of Sioux victories over government troops—against Custer at Little Bighorn. He is said to have captured three horses and a rifle in that battle.

The proud heritage of Chief Red Cloud lived on in his great-grandson, Edgar Red Cloud, who spent his early years with the old chief. When Edgar's mother died, he was sent to live with his great-grandfather. His Sioux education continued until Chief Red Cloud's death in 1909.

Edgar retained much of the information he learned while living with his famous great-grandfather and was able to relate the old Sioux legends as the original Red Cloud told them.

His early instruction covered how to pray to the Great Spirit, how to breed horses, the seasoning of wood and construction of bows and arrows, the breaking of ponies, translating animal calls, and the Sioux legends. He heard his great-grandfather tell of the battles with enemy tribes and the government soldiers. Edgar remembered seeing scalps that had been taken by his grandfather during these battles, and he eagerly listened to the story that went with each one.

His first lessons included the Sioux traditions of conservation. Young Edgar learned the Indian did not kill animals during the time they were raising their young. He was taught that buffalo should be killed only during the fall and early winter. This is the time they are fat and the hide is good.

Due to the teachings of his great-grandfather, the peace pipe always had an important meaning in Edgar Red Cloud's life. Prayers said with the peace pipe gave Red Cloud his strength, and he prayed with it daily.

Edgar recalled a story the old chief often would tell about the power of his peace pipe. During a battle with enemy Crow warriors, Red Cloud saw that his men were so outnumbered he feared all would be killed. The old chief dismounted from his horse and offered a prayer with his peace pipe. Resuming the fight, he led his Sioux soldiers to a great victory.

While making the treaty with the United States government, Red Cloud insisted that all those present smoke the peace pipe to show their good faith. "I want no one to fool my people; no forked tongue," Edgar Red Cloud quoted his great-grandfather as saying.

Talking about his great-grandfather, Edgar Red Cloud said the old chief was an Oglala Sioux of the Bear clan. The name Red Cloud was given to him when a ball of fire meteorite passed over Sioux country the night of September 20, 1822. According to old Sioux tradition, the infant is named for the first thing the mother sees after the child is born.

As a young man, Edgar Red Cloud applied the skills of horsemanship learned as a youngster to become a rodeo cowboy. During his rodeo career, he successfully rode a wild bison bull for the ten-second limit, a feat accomplished by very few men.

Later, he served on the Pine Ridge Reservation Tribal Council, as did his father, Jim Red Cloud. Edgar Red Cloud has maintained his family traditions by devoting a lifetime of service to his people.

LEGEND OF THE PEACE PIPE

Many moons before the first white settler came to the land of the Sioux, the most severe storm in history swept down from the northland.

Heavy snow blanketed the prairie, and icy winds had driven most of the buffalo far to the south. Game was difficult to find, and the food supply had dwindled to only a few pieces of jerky (strips of dried buffalo).

Many people were weak and dying from the bitter cold and famine. It was difficult to find enough strong men to go out and cut cottonwood to prepare as feed for the horses.

The chiefs called a meeting to decide what should be done. Some of the people wanted to search for a warmer land, but others feared such a move in the cold would cost many lives. Many of the tribe were very weak from lack of food.

After discussing the matter, they decided to send two of the strongest hunters out to see if game could be found to feed the people.

"With food, our people will be strong again," one chief told the others. "And with strength we can move out on the trail to search for the buffalo herds."

The hunters Big Bear and Red Horse were selected by

the chiefs. As they were leaving the camp, the hunters were told the success of their hunt was the people's last hope of survival.

Realizing this, the men expended all their strength looking for game. During the entire day they found only a small rabbit to show for their efforts. In their weakened condition, the pair knew they had to eat the small prize in order to make it back to camp.

Red Horse built a fire between two logs near the edge of a stand of pines. Over the coals they roasted the rabbit and shared the meat. The hot food gave them enough added strength to start the return trip.

As they were nearing their camp, Red Horse saw something headed toward them from a distant hill. Both men stopped and watched. Soon they could distinguish the figure of a beautiful maiden.

"What would a maiden be doing out here?" Big Bear asked.

"Let's wait and see what she wants," Red Horse replied. "Look! She's waving to us."

As the maiden approached, they could see that she was dressed in white buckskin and had a single white feather in her long braided hair. She carried a long-stemmed pipe decorated with white feathers.

"She is beautiful," Big Bear whispered to Red Horse. "She'd make a fine wife."

"The maiden is not looking for marriage," Red Horse said. "She is a sign that something wonderful will happen."

The maiden walked up to the hunters and addressed Red Horse. "I know you have hunted everywhere and were able to kill only a small rabbit. Your people are starving, and you need help. The Great Spirit sent me to give you this sacred peace pipe," the maiden said.

Red Horse, the older of the two, accepted the gift. As he examined it, she explained, "When your people are in need, you will clear your mind of all evil and offer a prayer in the four directions, north, east, south, and west. If you use the pipe with even one evil thought, you will be destroyed!"

Looking at Big Bear, she said, "I cannot marry. I was sent by the Great Spirit, and to think of marrying me is evil." Then she swung around and started to walk back toward the forested hills.

"But she needs a brave husband like me," Big Bear told Red Horse when she was beyond hearing range.

At that moment a large elk appeared and paused a short distance from the hunters. As they started to draw their bows, the elk suddenly disappeared.

"See there," Red Horse said. "You cannot think selfish thoughts. You must think of the peace pipe." Then a heavy fog rolled into the valley, and when it cleared, there was a pile of bones in the snow where Big Bear had been standing.

Red Horse returned to his people and reported what had happened. The chiefs looked at the pipe, which was made from a deer hoof. The leaders agreed that the Great Spirit had spoken, and from that time on, the Sioux people have used the peace pipe.

The original peace pipe, the Indians say, is kept by the Cheyenne River tribe. They only show it on special occasions and then only to those worthy to see it.

Telling of its power, the Sioux recall that one time three

men stole the original pipe. Within a few weeks all three had died. No one has tried to steal it since that incident.

LEGEND OF THE WIND CAVE

The American bison was the principal source of food for the Sioux Indians. In the fall when the animals were fat, tribal hunters would kill enough game to supply the tribe with meat through the winter.

It was on one of these fall hunts that Sioux hunters first reported seeing a herd led by a giant white buffalo. Over the years the hunters tried to catch the white buffalo, but because of his great size and speed, the Sioux horses would tire before a kill could be made.

One evening the tribal leaders met to devise a plan to take the great white buffalo. The chiefs decided to select two hunters who were both skilled and courageous, and to provide them with the strongest horses.

Carefully considering every hunter in the tribe, the chiefs agreed that White Antelope and Red Wolf should lead the hunt. These men were both great hunters. To make certain the chase would be successful, the chiefs directed other hunters to take extra horses and to station themselves on nearby hills. This would provide fresh horses if they were needed.

The next morning, White Antelope and Red Wolf located the great white buffalo and his huge herd. The pair carefully stalked the giant, and when almost within arrow range, the white buffalo started to run.

The hunters gave pursuit and after a grueling all-day chase, the Indians' horses began to tire. Changing to fresh mounts on a nearby hill, they were able to pick up the trail of their quarry quickly and resume the chase. The powerful bison led them into the Black Hills country.

A second change of horses enabled the hunters to close in on the animal. He was tiring, and the Sioux huntsmen were now within range. Several arrows found their mark. The great buffalo ran a short distance and collapsed. "What a prize we will bring back to our people!" thought the hunters.

But when White Antelope and Red Wolf arrived at the spot where they thought the white buffalo had fallen, he was not to be found. "How could an animal so large disappear before our eyes?" they asked. "Perhaps the Great Spirit is sending us a message."

Red Wolf slid off his horse. "I'm going to follow his tracks until I find him," he called to White Antelope. Seeing a trace of blood near the prints, Red Wolf knew the buffalo was nearby.

The tracks led to what appeared to be the entrance to a huge underground cave. Red Wolf soon discovered that a strong breeze flowed from this opening, and it was strong enough to blow his long braids straight up when he peeked over the edge.

Turning to his friend, he called, "White Antelope, come on. There's something here." Seeing that the tracks ended near the hole, the men decided their prize had disappeared into the earth. They debated whether or not it was safe to enter the windy cavern, but the desire to claim their trophy overcame their fears.

"If we can't get out all of our buffalo's carcass, maybe we can take part of it. We need only a piece of the hide to prove that our arrows were true," Red Wolf said. "I'll go down into the cave and look."

A long rope was made from strips of hide, and Red Wolf was lowered into the hole. But it was not quite long enough to allow him to reach the cavern. "It might be bad medicine to go deeper into the hole," White Antelope cautioned. Red Wolf agreed. They returned to the village for counsel after marking the hole with a pile of rocks.

The village chiefs did not find the story of the hunters believable. "These men must smoke the peace pipe so they speak with a straight tongue," one leader demanded. "Maybe killing the white buffalo put evil spirits into their hearts," said another. "Their story is to cover up failure," a third chief argued. "We must hear the truth."

So White Antelope and Red Wolf smoked the peace pipe, and all the chiefs sat in a circle around them to hear the truth. The hunters told the story of finding the hole, just as they had before.

"We must see this cave that makes much wind," the big chief told the others. "We must go to this place and look for the white buffalo."

The group of chiefs found the cave after a two-day journey. Using longer and sturdier ropes, they lowered some men down through the hole and into the cavern. Deep in the cave, the party found the bones of many buffaloes. But they could find no trace of the great white buffalo.

Later, a scout located the huge animal's unmistakable tracks leading from another entrance. Near the tracks were the four bloodstained arrows the hunters had used during the chase. The elusive white buffalo had escaped once again. But because the hunters had come so close to making a prize of him, he had left them a gift of a cave that could blow strong winds.

The chiefs decided that the great white buffalo had earned his freedom. To hunt him now would bring bad medicine to their people. Instead, they would accept his gift of the Wind Cave in the sacred Black Hills.

This legend has been handed down by the Oglala Sioux from generation to generation. It was told to Edgar Red Cloud by Chief Red Cloud himself, and points out the deep meaning the South Dakota Black Hills hold for the Sioux people.

The Wind Cave was made a National Park in 1903. The strong winds that blow alternately in and out of its mouth are caused by outside changes in atmospheric pressure.

LEGEND OF CRAZY HORSE

Chief Jack Red Cloud, Edgar's grandfather, rode into several battles with the famous Sioux war chief Crazy Horse. Just before his death in 1918, Jack Red Cloud told Edgar the famous Crazy Horse Legend and said he had actually witnessed the miracle.

Crazy Horse was always known to carry a flint rock in a buckskin bag. The flint was very hard and almost impossible to break. Even the strongest brave had difficulty in breaking it with a heavy hammer.

Before going into battle, Crazy Horse would remove the flint rock from the bag and bite off a piece of flint. After chewing it like candy, he would mix the finely chewed pieces with dirt from a gopher's mound and smear the mixture over both himself and his horse.

Then, leading his warriors, he would charge directly into the enemy. Cavalry soldiers shot at him many times, but their bullets never hurt him. When he was attacking enemy Indian tribes, tomahawk blows by enemy warriors would only bounce off, and their arrows could not penetrate the powerful medicine of the flint.

Many others tried to chew the flint rock, but it only damaged their teeth. The magic of the flint used by Crazy Horse could not be duplicated.

He told young men the power of the flint came to him in a vision. Crazy Horse would use the flint to recruit warriors. "I am a medicine man with a powerful protective medicine," he would announce. "If it hadn't protected me, I would have been killed by cavalry guns long ago. Even my horse is protected."

Many years have passed since the days of war chief Crazy Horse, but his legend is still being told. Old-timers living on the Pine Ridge Reservation in South Dakota say that the "vision of the flint" is the reason Crazy Horse became a great leader of the Sioux people.

III.

Sitting Bull Legends

As told by Frank White Buffalo Man

Few Indians have received greater recognition for their role as a war chief than Sitting Bull, one of the Sioux leaders credited with masterminding the smashing defeat of the United States Cavalry on the Little Bighorn battlefield.

At fourteen years of age, he demonstrated his desire to become a warrior by killing and scalping his first victim. As a reward, his father, who was called Sitting Bull, changed the boy's name from Jumping Badger to Sitting Bull. It was a great honor to bear the name of one's father.

As the youth matured, he took a position of leadership in his band. To his followers, Sitting Bull was considered a medicine man with divine powers. They believed his powerful medicine gave spiritual strength to those who followed his teaching.

Sitting Bull practiced the traditional Sioux philosophies and customs and held that the Black Hills were sacred land. The stampede of prospectors and settlers migrating into these hallowed hunting grounds inflamed him into action. For Sitting Bull, this was cause for revenge.

Before and during the Civil War, Chief Sitting Bull and his band carried out numerous raids on settlers, Crow war-

44

riors, and troop expeditions. On one of these skirmishes, Sitting Bull, after being wounded in the foot, killed a Crow chief. This act of courage impressed the Sioux Secret Warrior Society and eventually led to his nomination as head chief of the nontreaty Sioux hostiles.

The nontreaty hostiles needed a man who could bring them together in a common battle against the encroachments of the white man and enemy tribes. Following a series of tests and conferences, the chiefs of the various hostile bands elected Sitting Bull as head chief and installed him as their leader in public ceremonies.

Chiefs who pledged allegiance by smoking the peace pipe with the new head chief included the famous Hunkpapa Sioux Gall, Four Horns, Running Antelope, Red Horn, and Loud-Voiced Hawk. Oglala Chief Crazy Horse and his large band cast their lot with Sitting Bull, as did nontreaty Miniconjou, Sans Arc, and Cheyennes.

At about the time the hostiles consolidated under Sitting Bull, the government ceded considerable lands to the Sioux in order to satisfy the demands of Red Cloud. Earlier victories over the army had gained special concessions for Red Cloud in the Treaty of 1868.

Hearing of this treaty, Sitting Bull declared his group preferred to live without having the dictates of the white man forced upon them. As a final effort to bring about peace, the Catholic missionary Father DeSmet made a daring visit to the Powder River village of Sitting Bull. The Black Robe was welcomed by the nontreaty hostiles, but they did not respond to his suggestion of peace. Past experience had taught them that white man's government did not keep treaty promises.

George Armstrong Custer's August, 1874, report of "Immense Quantities of Gold and Silver in the Black Hills" brought a new rash of prospectors. The nonagency hostiles moved to repulse the waves of gold-seeking trespassers who violated the Red Cloud Treaty.

Hoping to eliminate hostile action while negotiating for rights to the Black Hills, the government ordered Sitting Bull's Indians to report to their respective agencies or face military action. This order not only strengthened Sitting Bull's position of leadership, but caused hundreds of young agency Indians to leave their reservations to join the hostile forces.

Sitting Bull ordered a huge Sun Dance Ceremony in mid-June, 1876, so that his people could communicate with Wakan Tanka, the Great Spirit. Taking the role of the chief dancer, he promised one hundred pieces of his flesh for divine guidance. In preparation for this ceremony, a medicine man was reported to have cut fifty small pieces of flesh from each of Sitting Bull's arms.

When the blood-caked chief finally collapsed from the hot rays of the sun and a day and a half of dancing without food or water, he whispered to those who gathered around him that he had experienced a divine vision. He told of seeing waves of charging cavalry, and as the soldiers approached him, they fell like grasshoppers.

The announcement of Sitting Bull's vision brought renewed confidence to the warriors. To them, the Great Spirit had spoken, and a great victory would soon be theirs.

Word of Sitting Bull's "Vision of Victory" spread

rapidly across the plains, bringing many volunteers to fight with the hostiles. The nontreaty Indians' ranks soon swelled to an estimated six thousand.

Following the victory over General Crook in the Rosebud River Valley, Sitting Bull moved his forces to a camp on the west bank of the Little Bighorn River. This new camp extended over two miles.

Elements of the 7th United States Cavalry sighted the hostiles' village on the evening of June 25, 1876, and the next morning Lieutenant Colonel George Armstrong Custer divided his force of six hundred men and launched an attack.

Sitting Bull was not that easy to take by surprise. Nearly two thousand warriors were waiting for the approaching soldiers. When the smoke of combat cleared, Custer and some 250 of his troopers lay dead on the field of battle to immortalize "The Last Stand" as a historical highlight in the Western movement. Realizing the military would seek revenge, Sitting Bull escaped into Canada. He remained in exile until July 18, 1881, when he surrendered to American Forces at Fort Buford, North Dakota. Nine years later he was killed by Indian police at his home on the Standing Rock Reservation.

Like most great Indian leaders, Sitting Bull placed unswerving faith in the lessons taught by tribal legends. He used the legends to teach Sioux traditions, and until his death in 1890, he resisted all attempts by government agents to change the culture of his people.

Passed on from parent to child, many of the stories once told by Sitting Bull have survived the influence of civilization. Frank White Buffalo Man, a grandson of Sitting Bull, retold stories that delighted him as a youngster. He emulated his famous grandfather by dedicating his life to preserving Sioux legends, customs and dances for future generations.

Until his death in 1977, Chief White Buffalo Man was a professional artist, capturing details of the past on canvas. But the tranquillity of an artist's studio did not dominate his search for adventure.

After completing his education at the Salem Indian School in Chemawa, Oregon, he was intrigued by the glamour of show business and joined Buffalo Bill's Wild West Circus. This led to performances with the traveling 101 Ranch Wild West Show and the Dunhamel Sitting Bull Swing Pageant, where he became the world's champion butterfly dancer, rope spinner, and cowboy artist.

He appeared in Western movies and toured the rodeo circuits. Despite his varied interests, Chief White Buffalo Man followed the cultures taught in legends told him as a boy. In them, he found strength to face problems of everyday life.

IKTOMI AND THE DUCKS

Iktomi, the spider, was the world's greatest trickster. He had a reputation for changing his form to deceive his victims.

Early one morning, when Iktomi went to the river for a drink, he noticed a flock of ducks swimming in the deeper water. Duck meat would make a wonderful breakfast, thought Iktomi. I must think of a plan to catch those ducks.

Iktomi knew the fox was a very cunning animal and very good at catching ducks. "I'll change myself into a fox, and then I can catch all the ducks I can eat," Iktomi said to himself. In an instant he became a fox.

"Hello, there," the newly formed fox yelled to the ducks. "Swim closer to shore so that I can talk to you."

"You can't fool us," the ducks replied. "We know you're Iktomi."

"You ducks are very observant," Iktomi answered. "And much too wise for me to fool."

The ducks were very self-satisfied to have outsmarted Iktomi. They discussed their feat and decided that, if Iktomi could not fool them, no one could. Iktomi, who had very sharp ears, overheard every word they said. They flatter themselves and will be easy to trick, he thought.

Iktomi called to the ducks again: "I'm not quick-witted enough to fool you, and it's useless to try. You have cleverly detected my finest trick, so I'll depart and wish you well. But before I leave, I feel it's my duty as a friend to warn you about the reflection of the bright morning sun off the water. It can be very dangerous for one's eyesight."

"What makes you say that?" the alarmed ducks called back.

"I wouldn't want to worry you, but I heard about a flock of ducks who failed to heed this warning, and their eyes turned red," Iktomi replied. "Fortunately I know a way to prevent this terrible thing from happening." After making that statement he turned and started to walk away from the river.

"Wait, wait," screamed the ducks. "Please tell us how to keep our eyes from turning red."

Iktomi returned to the riverbank. He stood silently for a moment, as if he were in deep thought. "Well, all right, since you're my good friends," he answered. "But I don't like to waste words. If I tell you, then you must promise to heed my advice."

By this time the ducks were very concerned for their eyes and promised Iktomi they would do just as he suggested. After all, was he not now a good friend?

"You must close your eyes tightly, then the glare will not turn your eyes red," Iktomi advised.

"Sitting out here on the river with our eyes closed all morning will become very tiresome," the ducks complained.

"Then why don't you dance?" Iktomi suggested. "Dancing with your eyes closed is a wonderful way to spend the morning. Since you are my friends, the least I can do for you is to stay and sing a song for your dance."

As Iktomi sang, all the ducks tightly closed their eyes and danced across the water. Closer and closer they danced to the place where the trickster was standing. When the ducks danced within reach, Iktomi grabbed them one by one and stuffed them into his sack.

Some of the dancers heard the commotion made by ducks fluttering in his sack and opened their eyes. Then they saw they had been tricked. "Open your eyes! Open your eyes! If you don't, Iktomi will kill you," they warned.

The remaining ducks managed to escape, but this trickery left a lasting mark on all waterfowl. That is why they are so wary today.

The Maiden Who Lived with the Wolves

The early Sioux Indians moved camp frequently when they were traveling to their summer hunting grounds. The journey from the winter camp to the summer area was many miles and took months of travel.

During these expeditions, the people carried most of their food supplies. When game and other edibles found along the trail became scarce, the Indians would use food from their reserves. If wild fruit and berries were plentiful in an area, sometimes the migrating band would camp nearby to replenish their food supply.

It was on such a halt that a young maiden decided to leave the camp for a few hours to gather food. Once away from the camp, she became lost and could not find her way back. After several days of wandering about, the young maiden finally found the campsite, but her people had struck their tepees and departed, leaving her to survive by her own means.

She was terrified as to what the future might hold, so she sat down on a large rock to calm her nerves and to think out a plan. While she was seated there, a large wolf walked by and sensed that she was very worried.

He felt sorry for her and came to her side. At first the girl thought he would attack, but his friendliness overcame her fears. She followed him to the top of a high butte, where the wolves of that region had their den.

The wolves seemed to welcome her, and she made her home with them. Soon she began to understand their ways and then their language. They learned to understand her ways too.

When she was hungry, the maiden would tell the wolves, and they would send a hunting pack to the valley to kill a buffalo for her. They would then drag the best pieces of meat up to the den for the maiden to eat.

The maiden lived with the wolves through the cold winter months. Early the next spring she looked down on the valley below and noticed a band of Indians had set up a camp. She asked the wolves to scout the camp to see if they were her people.

The scouting party returned to report the Indians camped below were her people. She thanked them for taking care of her and departed to the valley.

At the camp she had a joyful reunion with her people and told the story of how wolves had saved her from starvation and cold. She revealed how wolves shared responsibilities, stalked their prey, and hunted as a pack.

"We can learn from the wolves," the chief told his people after listening to the maiden's story. "When our hunters kill an animal for themselves, they can kill another for those who are unable to hunt. All will benefit, and our hungry elders, widows, and children will always have a source of food."

This plan was passed on from band to band until it became a practice of the Sioux people. The lessons gained from the experiences of the maiden who lived with the wolves provided a way to feed many who were unable to hunt for themselves.

LEGEND OF THE HORSE

Many moons ago, when the country was still young, Sioux Indians used dogs to help transport their belongings.

By hitching dogs to a pair of trailing poles joined by a frame, the Indians could move their heavy burdens. This type of vehicle is called a travois.

Only the most powerful dogs were used to draw the travois. Because the loads were heavy, the distance they could travel was very limited. This troubled the Indians, who longed for a faster way to move their possessions.

The chiefs held council to discuss this matter. "If our dogs were larger, our people could travel greater distances in a day," one said. "What we need is larger dogs."

"How will we find dogs that are larger," demanded a subchief. "We have a difficult time finding the buffalo."

The great chief rose and called for quiet. "We must pray with the White Buffalo Maiden peace pipe," he said. "Perhaps as the White Buffalo Maiden brought us the peace pipe from the Great Spirit, she might return to bring us a dog so large it could bear a man on its back. An animal that big could pull the travois with the power of a bull buffalo."

Early the following morning, the Sioux chiefs took their best peace pipe and asked the Great Spirit to send them an animal that would provide faster transportation.

They prayed: "We must be able to keep up with the great herds of buffalo. They are our most important source of food. When we lose contact with the buffalo, it is difficult for our people to catch up, and we face great hardships. Great Spirit, we need a dog that can outdistance the fastest buffalo. Then our people will have food and live in happiness."

After the prayers, the people started their watch for the return of the White Buffalo Maiden. But the days passed, and no matter how vigilant their watch was, the maiden did not appear. Nor was there any sign of a large dog.

Many of the Indians became very discouraged and said they thought the Great Spirit had not heard the prayers. Others said the prayers might not be answered because some tribal members were harboring evil spirits. Still others suggested that dogs that big didn't exist and that to pray for them was foolish.

The great chief told his people they must have faith. "I'm sure our prayers will be answered," he said and described a vision he had had during a dream. Through the vision he saw a great dog carrying a man on its back. The chief said the dog had hooves but different from those of a deer. It had a long mane and tail, and could run faster than the wind.

Some scoffed at the chief's vision. "It is just a dream," they said. "Who has seen a dog that looks like that?"

One day a strange-looking animal appeared on a hill overlooking the Sioux encampment. The people gathered in a line along the edge of their camp to watch this animal as it grazed. It was unlike any creature they had seen before, and for many this was a frightening experience. All agreed it must have been sent to them from the Great Spirit.

The next morning the animal entered the camp and

walked down the rows of tepees. "How do we catch this big dog?" the people asked the great chief.

When the animal entered the Sioux camp on the third day, the great chief took a piece of rope he had made from hides and captured it. Remembering his vision, the chief climbed upon the animal's back and learned to ride it. Then he trained it to pull a travois.

The people were amazed at how well the animal responded to training, and they praised the chief for his work. But he told them, "The Great Spirit spoke to me about this in a vision. I told many of you about it, but you lost faith, and some even scoffed. Now we have such an animal, and it is the gift of the White Buffalo Maiden and the Great Spirit. You should praise the Great Spirit for this sacred gift, not me."

The great chief officially named the animal Shunka Wankan, which means "sacred dog." For many moons the Sioux used Shunka Wankan to pull their travois and to ride on buffalo hunts. Because of Shunka Wankan's great speed, hunters could catch many more buffalo, and the people always had plenty to eat.

When the first pioneers ventured into Sioux territory, they said Shunka Wankan should be called horse and that their people originally brought horses to this country. But the Sioux remembered the Legend of the Horse and that Shunka Wankan was a gift to them from the Great Spirit.

LEGEND OF STANDING ROCK

One day a handsome Sioux chief called his band together and announced that he intended to take a second wife.

This made his first wife, an Arikara woman, very un-happy. Although he promised her she would be first in his heart, she became very jealous. No matter how he tried, he could not comfort her.

After the wedding took place, the Arikara woman re-fused to speak. When people spoke to her, she stared straight ahead and would not answer. She remained silent in her tepee.

It was time for the band to move to a new campground. The handsome young chief ordered the tepees struck and equipment packed. Everyone but his first wife responded to the order. Her friends tried to coax her to prepare to move, but she only sat in deep silence.

When her husband saw she was doing nothing to comply with his order, he became furious. "Woman, you must pack your things and prepare to move as I have ordered," he told her. "If you fail to do as I say, we will leave you here to starve." Despite his threat, she did not even flick an eyelash. Instead she sat as if she had not heard a word he had spoken.

The people completed packing and soon were ready to move. Only one tepee remained. "Your Arikara wife re-fuses to move," the people told the chief. "She prefers to stay here and die."

"Then we'll leave without her," the chief replied. "After a few hours of loneliness, she'll forget this foolishness." Raising his arm, the chief signaled the procession to start moving.

After the first night on the trail, the chief began to worry about his Arikara wife. He summoned his two brothers and told them, "Spending last night alone on the dark campgrounds should have brought your sister-in-law to her senses. I want you to go back and get that woman. Tell her to come. I'm afraid something might happen to her."

Realizing their brother, the chief, was very concerned for his wife, the brothers galloped their horses rapidly back to the deserted campgrounds. Their sister-in-law's tepee still stood alone near the center of the clearing. They noted her fire had burned out during the night.

She was still seated in her tepee. When they entered, she did not move. One of them said, "Sister-in-law, we came for you. Your husband, the chief, is very worried, and he wants us to take you back to him."

The pair waited anxiously for her reply, but there was none. She only sat staring straight ahead, as if she were a statue. One of the brothers edged close to her and touched the woman on the cheek. He rapidly withdrew his hand and yelled out, "She has turned to stone! Our sister-in-law has turned to stone."

Fearing it might be the work of an evil spirit, the brothers hurried back to their band. When they related the story to the chief and a medicine man, it was decided this might be a wonderful sign from the Great Spirit. They hurried to the tepee of the Arikara woman to see for themselves.

The medicine man carefully looked the situation over. Then he raised his hand and spoke. "What we see here was not caused by an evil spirit but is the work of the Great Spirit. By turning this woman to stone, the Great

Spirit has spoken. He says that wives must follow their husbands and made an example of this woman as a reminder."

The men fixed up a special travois for the stone woman, and wherever the band went, they took it with them. The people called the stone image Standing Rock.

Through the years, the Indians say, this stone has maintained its supernatural powers. Squaws who were experiencing problems in their married lives would visit Standing Rock for comfort and advice. This rock became very popular, and a large Sioux Indian reservation has been named after Standing Rock. At this time the stone is on a pedestal in front of the tribal office at Fort Chase, North Dakota.

IV.

Chief Joseph's Favorite
Nez Percé Legends

As told before the tragic Trail of Tears

One of the most incredible chapters to be recorded in all of Western history is the heartbreaking story of the non-treaty Nez Percé people and their struggle for freedom and peace.

That struggle was centered around the greatness of a single man, In-mut-too-yah-lat-lat, who was better known as Chief Joseph. Under his leadership, the Nez Percé made every effort to maintain peace. But once war was forced upon him, Chief Joseph and his warriors fought with unexcelled gallantry.

With a force that at no time numbered more than three hundred braves, the Nez Percé chief generaled a running battle with more than 1,900 trained United States troops over a trail that covered nearly two thousand miles. Outnumbered and in unfamiliar terrain, Chief Joseph had to take into consideration the safety of approximately 750 women and children and three thousand head of cattle when making his battle plans.

The Nez Percé met with federal troops eleven different times and engaged in battle on five occasions. Chief Joseph and his warriors compiled the remarkable record of three battles won against two defeats. It is interesting to note that, despite the bitterness of the war, Chief Joseph and his people conducted their military campaign without destruction of civilian property or the slaughter of innocent settlers.

Born the eldest son of the marriage of Old Chief Joseph and a Nez Percé squaw, young Joseph was destined to follow the example of his father. Old Joseph, whose Indian name was Teukakas, taught his young son the laws of the Nez Percé.

"No man can own any part of the earth, and a man cannot sell what he does not own," the old chief used to say. He taught young Joseph to treat all men as they treated him, never to be first to break a bargain, and that it was a disgrace to tell a lie.

When the rush for gold and the westward movement brought increasing numbers of squatters to lands used by the Nez Percé, Old Joseph began to show signs of passive animosity. He was disturbed that the whites would fence the land of his people, slaughter Indian stock without permission, and sometimes shoot at his Nez Percé tribesmen without reason.

The Treaty of 1855 established the Nez Percé Reservation, to include the present counties of Asotin in Washington, Wallowa in Oregon, Lewis, Nez Percé, and the western half of Idaho County in Idaho. But with the report of gold, more prospectors moved onto Nez Percé reservation land than there were Nez Percé Indians. Because of the mounting friction, the government proposed a revised treaty to protect the settlers.

Old Joseph, chief of the Wallamwatkin band that controlled the area near Lake Wallowa, Oregon, refused to sign. "The land is not mine to sell," he insisted. The hills around the lake supported rich grass for the ponies, and the waters teemed with fish. His people did not want to give up their homeland.

Failing to secure support of Joseph's Nez Percé, the government signed the Treaty of 1863 with Idaho Nez Percé bands. This treaty also included the sale of Joseph's Wallowa lands. Hearing of the treaty, both Old and Young Joseph refused to accept its terms, insisting they had declined the agreement.

Young Joseph took over more of a leadership role in governing his band, as blindness slowly darkened his father's eyesight. Finally, the old chief summoned his son to his bedside. He knew death was near.

The young chieftain grasped his father's hand as the old chief softly spoke. "My son, my body is returning to my mother earth, and my spirit is going very soon to see the Great Spirit Chief. In a few more years the white men will be all around you. They have their eyes on this land. My son, never forget my dying words. This country holds your father's body. Never sell the bones of your father and mother." (Joseph's own story, 1879.)

Young Joseph pressed his father's hand and promised he would protect the grave with his life. The old chief smiled and passed away. He was buried in the valley of Winding Waters in Wallowa, Oregon.

As time passed, Old Joseph's deathbed prophesy became a reality. Many land squatters were settling in northeastern Oregon, claiming large chunks of the Wallowa Nez Percé territory.

Frequent incidents between the Indians and settlers posed

a serious threat to Joseph's course of peace. The newly arriving squatters and gold-seeking prospectors stole large numbers of the Nez Percé's finest horses. Cattlemen settling in the valley branded the Indians' cattle and claimed them as their own. Disputes over ownership of land and stock became daily occurrences, and tensions on both sides peaked.

Increased pressure by government agents and threats of military intervention caused Joseph to travel to Fort Lapwai, Idaho. There, he was shown the reservation and given thirty days to round up the stock and move from Wallowa to Lapwai.

"Our stock is scattered, and we cannot round them up in thirty days," Joseph argued. "Your demands are without reason."

General Howard, representing the United States government, replied, "If you let the time run over one day, my soldiers will be there to drive you onto the reservation, and all your cattle outside of the reservation at that time will fall into the hands of the white man."

Joseph had resolved to remain at Wallowa, where his father was buried. The Treaty of 1863, which established the reservation at Fort Lapwai as the home of most Nez Percé bands, turned the Wallowa Valley over to the land squatters.

The young Wallowa Nez Percé chief was a great orator and often was able to hold the government negotiators at bay in debate. Typical of his skill in communicating his side of the argument was this explanation of the Treaty of 1863.

"Suppose a white man should come to me and say, 'Joseph, I like your horses, and I want to buy them.' I say to him, 'No, my horses suit me, I will not sell them.' Then he goes to my neighbor, and says to him: 'Joseph has some good horses. I want to buy them, but he refuses to sell.' My neighbor answers, 'Pay me the money, and I will sell you Joseph's horses.' The white man returns to me and says, 'Joseph, I have bought your horses, and you must let me have them.' If we sold our lands to the government, this is the way they were bought. On account of the treaty made by other bands of Nez Percés, the white men claim my lands."

When large numbers of troops were reported moving into his area, Joseph knew he was faced with the decision of resisting the move to Fort Lapwai or moving in peace. The younger men of his band demanded reprisals and war. But Joseph, although his father's dying words still rang in his ears, declared his people would move in peace.

Joseph told of his decision by saying: "I said in my heart that, rather than have war, I would give up my country. I would rather give up my father's grave. I would give up everything rather than have the blood of white men upon the hands of my people."

But Joseph's dream of peace was to be shattered. As he led his people to the reservation, several of his young braves conducted a raid, killing four settlers. This act touched off the war of 1877.

From the Wallowa Valley to the Bearpaw Mountains, his running fight with the United States Army was a personal Trail of Tears for Chief Joseph. His beloved brother Allokut was killed during the Bearpaw Mountain battle, and earlier two of his wives were shot by soldiers at the Big Hole encounter.

As a condition of surrender, the U.S. Army promised

Joseph that his people would be returned to the reservation at Fort Lapwai, Idaho. But after the surrender he and his band were exiled to Fort Leavenworth, Kansas, where malaria and other diseases claimed the lives of many. When the number of Nez Percé survivors had dropped to only 268 men, women, and children, the government authorized their return to the Northwest.

The remnants were divided into two groups. Chief Joseph and 150 of his people were sent to Nespelem, Washington. The remaining 118 rejoined loved ones who lived at Lapwai, Idaho.

With the exception of a few visits east and one to the University of Washington campus, Chief Joseph lived out his remaining years at Nespelem. Death called the famous warrior September 21, 1904, and he was buried at Nespelem.

He died without the benefit of a single grandchild. Although he fathered nine children, only one, Sarah Moses, survived to marriageable age. His daughter Sarah did marry, but the union was without children.

Today, the only descendants of Chief Joseph are great-nieces or -nephews. Joseph had two sisters (Sarah Conners and Celia), and most of his survivors can be traced through them.

Coyote and the Monster

Near the beginning of time, before there were people and when all animals spoke a common language, a huge monster named Iltswetsix roamed the valleys of the winding waters.

The monster was very ugly, with huge front teeth, small

Paul Leschi (1889-1980), grandson of Quiemulth and grandnephew of Nisqually Chief Leschi, recalled stories once told by his famous ancestors. This collection was revealed for the first time since Paul Leschi was taught the legends by his dying grandmother in 1898. He retold each story in his native tongue and then made a line-by-line translation for the author. (Photo by author)

The body of Chief Leschi now rests in this grave at the Tacoma Indian Cemetery, Tacoma, Washington. Chief Leschi originally was buried near what is now Fort Lewis. Expansion of the facilities for World War I forced Nisqually tribesmen to move the body before construction workers destroyed the burial site. (Photo by author)

Chief Red Cloud, the Ogalala Sioux leader who consolidated Oglala power. His Sioux name was Mahpiya Luta or Scarlet Cloud. This picture was taken by Charles M. Bell in 1880. (Photo courtesy Smithsonian Institution National Anthropological Archives, Bureau of American Ethnology Collection) Insert pictures Chief Red Cloud's grave at Holy Rosary Mission, South Dakota.

We-tamahecha or Lean Woman, wife of Chief Red Cloud. Photographer was James Mooney of the Bureau of American Ethnology. Photo taken in 1893. (Courtesy Smithsonian Institution National Anthropological Archives, B.A.E. Collection)

Chief Jack Red Cloud, son of Chief Red Cloud who fought with Chief Crazy Horse at the Little Big Horn. Date of this photograph was not recorded. (Courtesy Smithsonian Institution National Anthropological Archives, B.A.E. Collection)

Chief James Red Cloud
Grandson of Chief Red Cloud who gave many years of service to Pine Ridge Reservation. Photo courtesy of Smithsonian Institution National Anthropological Archives, Bureau of American Ethnology Collection.

Chief Edgar Red Cloud, great grandson of the famous chief who brought the Ogalala together to form a nation. He reached back into his memory seven decades to recall legends and stories often told by his great grandfather.

A ranger examines the "boxwork" formations at the Wind Cave, Wind Cave National Park, South Dakota. Strong currents of air blow alternately in and out of the cave and they are believed to be caused by changes in atmospheric pressure. "The Legend of the Wind Caves" tells how the Sioux first discovered the cave and its strange phenomenon. (National Park Service photo)

A Sioux camp photographed by Alexander Gardner near Fort Laramie in the Dakota Territory during treaty negotiations with Chief Red Cloud in 1868. (Courtesy Smithsonian Institution National Anthropological Archives, B.A.E. Collection)

Chief Sitting Bull (1834-1890). Medicine man and warrior best known for his role in the Battle of the Little Bighorn. Photo courtesy South Dakota State Historical Society.

Sitting Bull's wives and daughters photographed outside their log cabin at Grand River. Courtesy Smithsonian Institution National Anthropological Archives, B.A.E. Collection.

Frank White Buffalo Man, a grandson of Sitting Bull, recalled legends once told by his famous grandfather to make up the Sitting Bull collection published in this book. Photographs taken by the author in 1969. It is interesting to note that Chief White Buffalo Man never allowed himself to be photographed with his eyes open.

Chief Joseph (extreme right) pictured with three unidentified members of his band. Photograph was taken well before the War of 1877, probably in the later 1860's or early 1870's. Courtesy Smithsonian Institution National Anthropological Archives, negative 56,600.

Chief Joseph with General Gibbon on the shore of Lake Chelan in Washington State. Photograph was taken in 1889. Courtesy Smithsonian Institution, B.A.E. Collection. Negative 43,201.

Hinmaton Yalatkit or Chief Joseph, the Nez Perce general who led his people in the hard-fought War of 1877, posed for this F. J. Haynes photograph at Bismark, Dakota Territory in 1877. Photo courtesy of The Smithsonian Institution negative 43,201-A.

Tall-Kin-Kin-My, great-niece of Chief Joseph (1914-1982). Assisted in the collection and authentication of her great-uncle's favorite Nez Perce Legends. Photo by author.

Whea—Kadim (1870-1938) who took the name William Shelton at the Tulalip Indian Mission School. Chief Shelton was dedicated to improving schools on the reservation.

Totem-style story pole carved by Chief William Shelton. It stands in front of the Tulalip Reservation School. (Photo by author)

Harriet Shelton Dover, daughter of Chief Shelton, is pictured above as a Miss Indian Washington contestant in 1938 and as she posed for the author in 1969.

Arnold Hunter and his mother, Helma Swan Ward, grandson and daughter of Makah Chief Charlie Swan. The blanket worn by Arnold Hunter was the one used by his grandfather. Ceremonial masks have been handed down for generations in the chief's family and are reported to be well over one hundred years old. Helma Ward translated the Makah legends for this book. Photo taken by author in 1969.

Yalocub, popular hereditary chief of the Makah. Born in 1880, he was widely known as Chief Charlie Swan. Chief Swan was a talented speaker and he possessed a special ability for putting across ideas. (Photo supplied by family).

Gwakotsa, who was known as Susie Peters among white settlers. This photograph of Chief Sampson's mother was taken at the Belole Longhouse January 1938. Gwakotsa saw nearly a century of change in her people and the land that supported them. Photo courtesy of family.

Chief Martin Sampson (1888-1980) often is referred to as the dean of Northwest Indian storytellers. He dedicated his life to the preservation of the Puget Sound Indian culture. Photo by author in 1967.

ears, a fierce temper, and a ravenous appetite. His long sharp claws were feared by all the creatures of the world, because he would seize anyone who came near him. Once a victim was in the grasp of his claws, there was no chance for escape. The monster either ate or drowned them all.

The waters of this area held more than enough fish for both the monster and the animals. But the monster decided to stop the animals from fishing.

"I want to have all the fish for myself, and you shall have none," he announced.

Soon the animals became very hungry. Something had to be done about the monster, so they held a great meeting of all the creatures. "We must persuade the monster to allow us to fish or we will all starve," one told them. "We must send one of our leaders to explain our need for fish."

The animal selected to meet with the monster had great courage. He went to the edge of the water very near the huge creature. "The fish were put in these waters to feed all of us. It's not right that you should deny anyone when fish are so plentiful," he said. "The animals beg of you— share the fish with us, or we will surely starve."

"I cannot grant your request," the monster told the animal spokesman. "If I allowed you to fish, your great hunger might compel you to catch every one before your stomachs were satisfied, and then there would be none left for me." After making this reply, he seized the spokesman and devoured him.

News of the famine soon spread across the land to the coyote, who in those days was a special type of animal. He was known as the changer, because he was working to prepare the world for great changes.

Coyote announced he knew of the hardships the animals suffered at the hands of the monster and promised to destroy it, although he didn't know how he could accomplish his promise. He knew it would be a very difficult task. Many had tried before him, and all had ended up in the monster's stomach.

Coyote went deep into the forest to concentrate on a plan. Seated beside a large rock, he thought and thought. Wise as he was, he couldn't devise a way to slay the monster. While he was worrying about this, his cousin the fox happened along the trail. "What are you doing up here?" Fox asked.

"I'm seeking wisdom to destroy the monster," Coyote replied. "Do you know of a way?"

"I could tell you what to do," Fox said. "But if I do, you'll say you had thought of my suggestion already." Fox refused to cooperate further.

The crafty coyote knew his cousin was terrified of lightning and thunder. Looking at the sky, he called up to the heavens, "Lightning and Thunder, come down and strike those who will not help."

"Stop, stop," pleaded the frightened fox. "I'll help you if you don't bring on Lightning and Thunder." Fox then outlined a plan for the destruction of the monster.

When Fox finished explaining his plan, Coyote stood up and said, "My cousin, the plan you've just suggested is the same one I had planned to use all along."

Following the advice of Fox, Coyote made a long spear and wrapped most of the shaft and handle with a strong cord. Placing a loop of cord around his wrist, he went looking for the monster.

Before the monster could seize him with its sharp claws, Coyote plunged his spear into its side. The monster roared and plunged to the depths of the waters, dragging Coyote behind him. During the struggle that followed, all the water spilled out of the valley and cut a deep channel as it raced to the bitter waters of the ocean.

The monster and Coyote fought, rolling over and over. As they tumbled, they made wide places and deep canyons in the channel. When they reached the ocean's breakers, the monster was very angry. He was killing and swallowing everything he saw.

The monster still had its great strength, and Coyote was becoming very tired. He'd have to resort to his cunning in order to win over the monster. Coyote swam to the beach for rest and to devise a new plan.

After thinking and thinking, Coyote couldn't think of a plan that would befit his cunning reputation. So he sat and waited for help.

Muskrat, who had been watching the fight from the beach, hurried to Coyote's side. "Maybe together we can kill the monster," Muskrat volunteered.

"He is too large and powerful," Coyote said. "We need a plan to use my magic and my cunning."

Muskrat, noticing the monster was nearing the beach and might overhear the conversation, whispered a plan into Coyote's ear. When Muskrat had finished explaining the last detail, Coyote said, "The plan you have just suggested is the same one I already planned to use."

Coyote, following Muskrat's suggestion, went to the edge of the breakers and turned himself into a branch of a tree. When the outgoing tide carried him to the monster, it opened its jaws and swallowed him whole. Once in the monster's stomach, he turned himself back into a coyote and used a stone knife to cut the heart out of the monster. The knife had been a present from the muskrat.

Muskrat helped Coyote beach the dead monster. Then the pair sat down to decide what to do with its remains.

"From the body of Iltswetsix we will make a new race of people," Coyote announced. Together they cut the monster into pieces, and when the pieces had been spread across the land, Coyote then changed each piece into a tribe of people.

The mighty head of the monster became the Nez Percé tribe. "These people shall occupy the Wallowa Valley and command all the surrounding territory," Coyote decreed. "The Nez Percé people shall have the brains and be a people of great counsel. They will make great herders and warriors, and be taller, stronger, and nobler than the others."

Coyote then created other new people to settle the areas near the Big River (the Columbia) that had been formed by the struggling monster.

The monster's legs were turned into the Blackfeet tribe. They were given lands east of the Shining Mountains (the Rockies), where the buffalo lived. The arms and claws of the monster were used to create the Cayuse Indians, who became skillful in the use of the bow and arrow. They settled along the Big River.

The skin of the monster became the Flathead Indians, who would be distinguished by complexions that were lighter colored than those of other tribes. The body was transformed into the Yakimas, who would occupy the valleys and plains to the north.

Finally, Coyote had only the heart left. He held it aloft, trying to think of what people he should make next. The Great Spirit, who was well pleased with Coyote's work, called down from the clouds, "You have done well, Coyote. To remind the people of your wonderful deeds, I will turn the heart into a huge stone for all to see." The rock has endured the centuries and is still visible in northern Idaho.

The wild animals lost their ability to talk when the monster was killed. But to this day they remember that people were created from the monster that terrorized them many years earlier, and their fear still remains. That is why wild animals are so difficult for hunters to stalk.

The Serpent of Wallowa Lake

For many summers Nez Percé warriors went into the buffalo country to hunt buffalo. Members of the Blackfeet tribe also used the same hunting grounds.

During one hunt, the Nez Percé chief and some of his warriors were attacked by a large force of Blackfeet. In the battle that followed, many Nez Percé were killed and scalped.

The Nez Percé vowed that the hostile acts of the Blackfeet would be avenged. During the cold winter months, the Nez Percé prepared for war. They made great quantities of arrows, bows, and spears for warriors who would seek revenge.

Late that next summer, the warriors departed for the buffalo hunting grounds. There, they met the Blackfeet in battle once more, but this time the Nez Percé were strong and won a great victory. They killed many Blackfeet braves and captured most of their horses.

Year after year the Nez Percé and Blackfeet tribes met and fought. Each time the Nez Percé warriors would be the victors, driving the Blackfeet from the buffalo range east of the Great Mountains.

One year, the Nez Percé took a large number of women and children into the buffalo country. Not having located any Blackfeet during the journey, the entire band slept during the night without benefit of a guard. That night, a large number of Blackfeet warriors crept into the Nez Percé camp and killed many warriors, women, and children while they slept. Those that survived had to retreat to the Nez Percé village. The trip was long, and on the trail the battles were many. Every warrior was exhausted.

The Blackfeet knew the Nez Percé were in a weakened condition. They wanted to continue the attack, but the sun was low in the west.

Because of the darkness, the Blackfeet postponed attack until morning. Then they would overrun the Nez Percé village and kill every man, woman, and child. To celebrate this occasion, the Blackfeet built large fires and danced to the traditional victory songs.

The Nez Percé chief had a beautiful daughter. She was admired and respected by her tribe, and she, in return, loved her people. Word of her great beauty had spread across the land, and she would make a fine prize for the Blackfeet.

The maiden knew her father and his warriors could not withstand the attacks the dawn would bring. She thought she must act to save her people, so she quietly slipped through the sleeping village to her canoe. The princess silently launched the craft and carefully paddled to the camp of the Blackfeet. Without making a sound, the princess beached her canoe and crept through the rows of enemy tepees until she found the largest fire. This must be the fire of the head chief, she thought.

The maiden walked straight to the Blackfeet warrior, who was decorated with several fresh Nez Percé scalps. Her courage almost failed as she approached him, and her lips momentarily trembled with fear. "I am the daughter of the Nez Percé chief," she announced. "I have come to speak to the great chief of the Blackfeet."

The tallest of the warriors looked at her. "I am the chief," he replied. "What does the Nez Percé princess wish to say?"

"My people do not know I am here. I must plead for them because our young warriors have all been killed. The women are mourning their sons and husbands who have fallen in battle. You have nothing to gain by attacking the elderly and the helpless. I urge you to return to the land of the Blackfeet without further bloodshed."

The chief took a step closer to the princess before answering. "You and your people do not deserve to live," he said. "We will not be happy until your camp is destroyed."

He pushed the maiden to the ground and drew back his spear to plunge it into her heart. His handsome young son stepped between his father's spear and the girl.

"If you must take a life, Father, I beg of you, take mine

instead of this girl's. Because she loves her people and shows great bravery in coming to our camp is not a reason to kill her. I no longer have heart to fight her people."

"Step aside, my son, for I must do my duty," the chief said. "This girl's people have taken many of my braves and have tried to destroy the Blackfeet. Now we must avenge their deeds."

The beautiful princess dropped facedown on the ground, expecting the Blackfeet chief to plunge his spear into her. As she lay waiting for the fatal blow, the chief's son spread his blanket over her. He again stepped between his father and the girl.

"Why do you place your blanket on this daughter of our enemy's chief, my son?" the father asked. "Remove it at once, for you bring disgrace to your family. Her father and her people are dogs."

The boy refused to move. "The Nez Percé are not dogs," he answered. "They have fought with a brave heart. Our warriors have chased them across the rugged mountains. Their braves were weak with hunger, yet they continued to fight hard without surrender. Now they have reached their village, and only a few remain. I say the Nez Percé are not dogs! I will leave my blanket on the girl."

The chief's son was a great warrior, and this made the father very proud. The older man's heart softened. "Your tongue speaks from the heart," he said. "I will place my blanket on yours."

The maiden was told she could return to her people unharmed, and her village would be spared from attack. As the girl was about to launch her canoe, the chief's son ran to the beach. "Wait," he called. "I must speak with you."

When the young man approached the maiden, he said, "Your great beauty is matched only by your brave heart. I have much to say. On the night of the fourth moon, listen for the song of the cricket. I'll meet you then by the edge of the lake, and I will speak my heart."

Returning to the village, the girl counted the moons until the night of the fourth. It was nearing midnight when she heard the chirp of a cricket. The young man had arrived.

Very quietly, she made her way through the village to the lake. There she met the Blackfeet chieftain's son.

He greeted her by saying that her great beauty made the danger of his visit worth the risk. Then he said, "Among my people I am considered a great warrior, and the maidens of my tribe seek my attention. But my heart will be satisfied with no one but you. I want you to be my wife."

"Since I first laid eyes on you, I knew you would make a fine husband," she replied. "But our marriage cannot be. My people would not approve. They are at war with the Blackfeet."

"Our people must live in peace," the young warrior told her. "Our marriage can show them the way. Six more moons will pass, and you will hear a coyote howl. If you will come once again to the lake's edge, I will speak again." Then he climbed into his canoe and slipped away into the darkness.

The maiden again counted the moons until six had passed. Then, as the young warrior had promised, she heard the wail of a coyote. At the edge of the water she found the Blackfeet chief's son waiting for her.

"My people have discussed our marriage," he reported.

"They say it will give our tribes a binding peace. My father and the other leaders wish to smoke the peace pipe and make friends of the enemy Nez Percé."

"I've spoken to my father and my people also. They say they'll let your people fish our lake, and you will allow our hunters to go into the buffalo country. We will always live in peace."

It was arranged that the chiefs should meet several days later. At the meeting, all sat around the campfire and smoked the peace pipe. Then the Blackfeet chief addressed the group.

"My son wishes to give his heart to the daughter of the Nez Percé chief. This is good. It means we will live in peace."

"My daughter's heart is with your son," the Nez Percé chief replied. "He may take her to your camp to be his wife."

A great wedding feast was held, the runners were sent to the other Nez Percé bands and to the Yakima and the Cayuse tribes. At the end of the feast, the newly married couple took a canoe out on the lake. As they were paddling toward the mountains, the waters suddenly seemed to boil.

The young couple tried to paddle their craft toward the shore, but strong currents in the troubled waters pulled them to the center of the lake. Small ripples grew into huge waves, and the horror-stricken people gathered along the shores saw the head of a huge serpent rise from the depths of the lake. It was black in color and had huge nostrils, and fire shot from its eyes.

It circled the young people's canoe; then with a splash

it swam over them, and the canoe and its occupants were never seen again. Members of both tribes searched the shoreline, but the bodies were never recovered.

A period of mourning and wailing was observed by both tribes, and the Blackfeet left for their own country. They felt the Great Spirit was angry with them for making peace with the Nez Percé and had punished them by taking away their popular young chief.

The Blackfeet never returned to the lake because they feared the Great Spirit might punish them a second time.

"We made peace with our ancient enemies, and we were punished," the Nez Percé chief told his people. "I encouraged this friendship and lost my daughter, who was both beautiful and brave. My heart is sad."

From that time to the advent of the white man the Nez Percé and the Blackfeet people have considered themselves enemies.

V.

Snohomish Lesson Legends

From the family of Chief William Shelton

The story of the late William Shelton, last hereditary chief of the Snohomish tribe, is a legend of inspiration for all who seek knowledge.

Reared in the traditional Indian way of life, he gained his early education from lessons taught in legends related by his parents. In 1923 Chief Shelton wrote of the deep meaning that lived in every legend of his childhood. Of them he said, "They told me stories which would create in me the desire to become brave and good and strong; to become a good speaker, a good leader, and they taught me to honor old people and to do all in my power to help them."

Chief Shelton's Indian name was Whea-Kadim, which means "one who seeks answers." He was born into a family whose background claimed many great leaders. Among them was an uncle, Steh-Salth, who is recorded in Washington State history as Tyee William. Whea-Kadim married the daughter of Shehopé, a highly respected chief who was known to the early Washington territorial government as General Pierce. Both Tyee William and General

Pierce were signers of the Point Elliot Treaty made with the United States in 1855.

When he was a small child, Whea-Kadim's family moved to Whidbey Island in Puget Sound to escape settlers homesteading the lands around the Mission Beach Village. Indians of that time feared diseases that came west with the settlers. They had little resistance even to common colds, and such diseases often swept through villages in epidemic proportions, killing many people.

Whea-Kadim's family lived in near isolation during his childhood years. During this period, he asked his father to explain the meanings of the totemlike carvings in the longhouse at nearby Sandy Point. His father explained that each carving represented a legend, and that each legend carried a lesson. In order to achieve greatness, he was told he must learn all the lessons.

As a youth, Whea-Kadim was groomed to be a great medicine man. With his foresight and ability to learn, his parents held great hopes that he would gain the power to cure even the most dreaded diseases.

But the lure of gaining knowledge enticed him to paddle his canoe across the choppy waters of Puget Sound in 1888 and to enroll in the Tulalip Indian Mission School. The eighteen-year-old youth felt that learning to speak, read, and write English would be important to the future of his people.

At the mission school, a priest gave him the name William Shelton. Several of his cousins had enrolled earlier, and they had adopted the name of Shelton. Young Whea-Kadim accepted this as his surname also.

During the next three years he would learn enough English to qualify later for the position of government interpreter and lay the foundation for a career of service on his reservation.

He was dedicated to working in behalf of his people, and as chief he was instrumental in helping Indians turn timber into income. A great believer in education, Chief Shelton worked to improve reservation schools. The Tulalip Reservation is still noted for its fine school system.

"The white man teaches the children to be kind, good, generous, honest, brave; and the old Indian teaching was exactly that, but explained by examples or stories," he once wrote. Shelton felt the legends learned as a youngster guided him throughout his life.

He made a lasting mark in Snohomish County and Washington State history. When he died in 1938, there were hundreds of cars in the funeral procession, carrying scores of famous men, both red and white; there were Indian women with bright shawls, and white women wearing expensive fur coats. The crowd was so large that it could not be accommodated in the small reservation clapboard church, and loudspeakers were set up on the lawn. It was the most talked-about funeral of the time.

And now, many years later, people still remember the boy who wanted an education so much that he braved the currents of Puget Sound in a small canoe to learn to read and write.

Chief Shelton is survived by a daughter, Harriet Shelton Dover, who lives on the Tulalip Indian Reservation near Everett, Washington.

"Snohomish tribal lands covered most of the area that

is now Snohomish County, extending from the town of Skykomish to the lower half of Whidbey Island," Mrs. Dover said in relating her tribe's history. From her childhood she remembered shredded-cedar-bark dresses—soft as fine cotton and water-repellent too. The cedar-bark dresses were worn for about two weeks and then burned, she said. Dressmaking was a continuing project for women.

"Evening was the quiet time," Mrs. Dover recollected. "The children had to keep their voices low, and jumping about was forbidden." To help remind youngsters that the evenings should be quiet, the legend of Sway-Uock was told and retold. Fearing the ugly witch, who was noted for seizing noisy children, youngsters living in Snohomish longhouses took great care to talk quietly after sunset.

Mrs. Dover clearly remembers her early social training. Her grandmother, who spoke no English, taught her manners, such as the proper way for a lady to walk into the longhouse. "To walk like a real Indian lady, we learned to take short steps, to hold our bodies erect, and we were instructed not to raise our knees high," she reminisced. Young girls also were taught to restrain loud laughter or giggling, to turn the head slowly at public meetings, and to sit with the knees together.

Each of the Snohomish legends told by Chief Shelton points out an important lesson. "Arrows and the Sun" reminds young men to heed their mother's advice. Because Young Chief Bead respected his mother's suggestion, he became the greatest man of his time. The legend of Doh-Kwi-Buhch tells the people of the world that they will accomplish more by working together than they could accomplish by themselves.

ARROWS AND THE SUN

At one time the sun was controlled by a powerful chief whose people lived in a small village near Puget Sound. So absolute was his control over the sun that he could make the sun shine both night and day.

The people of neighboring tribes and villages longed for such power, for the possession of the sun would provide them with heat and light, and they could use its rays to destroy their enemies.

Early one morning the powerful chief received a challenge to a shooting contest from Chief Far West, who was his brother-in-law. He proposed that the sun should be given to the man who could hit it with his first arrow. After thinking it over, the big chief decided to accept the challenge. He invited the finest marksmen to take part in the competition.

On the day of the contest, brave after brave carefully aimed and fired an arrow at the sun, but none was able to score a hit. Finally, Chief Far West, who had made the original challenge, stepped up with his bow and arrow. He sighted down the shaft, drew back his powerful bowstring, and sent an arrow straight to its mark. Ownership of the sun was passed to Far West. His tribe was overjoyed, for now they would always have heat and light. The fame of their chief's conquest spread across the land.

The people who had to give up the sun were very sad. They knew their way of life would become more difficult, as they were not used to working in darkness.

"We must take action to recover the sun by preparing

for a new contest," the defeated chief told his village. "Every brave who is strong enough to shoot an arrow to the sun must train for the new contest." The big chief promised to train even harder than the rest.

When the time came, the big chief called his tribesmen together and announced he would lead his marksmen to the land of Far West's tribe the next day. He was certain the sun would be returned, for he and his braves had worked very hard to be ready for this contest.

Once in Far West's camp, the big chief arranged for a new contest.

"My brother-in-law," Chief Far West said, "I'll be most generous with you. Instead of restricting you to the use of only one arrow, I'll permit you to use all of your arrows. If you can hit the sun, it is yours. If you fail, I will have you and your braves killed."

The big chief hesitated a moment and thought over Far West's offer. "We will abide by your ruling," the big chief finally replied, and the marksmen were taken to the spot from which they were to shoot at the sun.

Each archer took his place on the line and one by one fired his arrows. After the braves had completed their attempts, the sun remained untouched. Then the big chief, who had been carefully sorting his arrows while the others were shooting, stepped to the line. With care, he placed an arrow in position, drew his bow to its fullest, aimed, and fired. The arrow veered off into the clouds, missing the sun. The big chief tried a second and a third time, and again and again, until he had fired his last arrow. But he missed the sun each time.

"I'm sorry you missed," Far West said. "Now I must

carry out the terms of our agreement and kill you and your braves." He ordered the big chief and his men seized and placed on poles that offered little protection from the sun. Then the sun's hottest rays were directed on them, and in time they died.

Many days passed, and the people back at the village of the big chief feared misfortune had befallen their leader and his braves. So the big chief's son called a tribal meeting. After great debate, the people concluded their chief had been killed. Elders of the village urged their strongest young braves to prepare for a new competition. "The sun must be won back, and our chief's death avenged," they proclaimed.

The son, whose name was Young Chief Bead, was declared the new chief and appointed to lead an expedition to Far West's village. All the braves except Young Bead went into vigorous training. At the direction of his mother, he was sent into the forest for several days to prepare himself for the competition.

Young Chief Bead was not allowed to take food or water into the forest with him. At the end of the second day, when he was nearly exhausted from hunger and thirst, he found a large lake. There, Young Chief Bead was astonished to see a great totem appear from beneath the lake's surface.

"Don't be alarmed," the totem, who introduced himself as Skalaletaad, assured the young chief.

"I can do much for you. I'm prepared to extend powers that will help you win the sun from your uncle. But you must have faith in me, or you will destroy yourself," the totem explained. The youth promised to heed the advice of the totem.

The totem outlined suggestions for the youth to follow, including taking a small mouse with him to the competition. After the discussion, Young Chief Bead ran back to the village to tell his mother of the meeting. Later, he told all the people of his experience.

At first some of the people could not understand why a totem spirit would bother with such a young boy, and they doubted his word. But when they noticed the strange expression on the youth's face, they were convinced something special had happened to him.

In keeping with the totem's instructions, the young chief took a mouse with him when he left for the land of Far West.

At the village of Far West's tribe, Young Chief Bead was greeted by his uncle, who controlled the sun. "My nephew, I'm sorry you've come to risk your life and the lives of these fine braves. Many great men, far more skilled than you, have tried and lost. Please return to your village. I am sure it is impossible for you to succeed, and if you fail, I must take your life and the lives of your braves. This would cause great sorrow in my family."

The young chief insisted that he be accorded the same opportunity permitted others. "I know the penalty if I should fail," he told his uncle. "A brave man does not fear death."

The Far West Chief reluctantly took the lad and his party to the place from which they were to shoot. Once again he pleaded with the young chief not to attempt to win the sun, but the youth was determined.

While the uncle was urging the youth to change his mind, the tiny mouse made his way into the village.

There, he found many bodies hanging from stakes, one

of which he identified as the father of Young Chief Bead. With his newly discovered information, the mouse hurried back to tell the young chief.

Young Bead had not yet stepped up to the line when Mouse climbed up onto his shoulder. "My chief," squeaked the mouse, "the body of your father hangs among many others near the house of your uncle. I know you'll tax your skill to the utmost and win the sun for our people." Young Bead thanked Mouse for his encouraging words and prepared to fire an arrow at the sun.

Taking careful aim, the youth drew back his bowstring and fired. The shaft fell far short of its mark. Chief Far West stepped up to the line and told the youth, "Because you are my nephew, I will make an exception in your case as I did for your father. You may shoot all the arrows you have in your bag."

As the youth prepared to send a second arrow flying at the sun, Mouse urged the young chief to remember the power of the totem. This gave the young chief the encouragement needed to pull the bowstring a little farther back and the arrow struck the lower edge of the sun.

"My nephew, I'm proud of you," the uncle stated. "I'm happy you and your people have won the sun. Now I am ready for death, according to the agreement." Young Chief Bead ordered the braves to place the uncle on a stake, as had been done to his father and the others.

Then the young chief followed the mouse to the body of his father and removed it from the stake. "If only I could bring my father back to life," Young Chief Bead said to Mouse.

"Remember the song of the totem," reminded Mouse.

"Sing your totem song, and I will direct energy from the sun into his body."

The young chief summoned his braves and directed them to build a giant drum, then giving each a drumstick, he had them sit around the drum and beat a rhythm while he sang. As young Chief Bead chanted the song of the totem, the tiny mouse worked on the body of Great Chief.

Life slowly began to enter the father's body, and after many hours he opened his eyes. He smiled happily, and tried to talk, but the old chief was too weak. "Save your strength," Mouse cautioned. "There will be time for words later."

Young Chief Bead carried his father down to their canoe, making him as comfortable as possible before starting the long journey home. Mouse looked after the sun, directing it to follow as they paddled away.

Back at the village, people were anxious to learn the fate of the young chief. When they began to fear he had suffered the same misfortune that befell his father, one noticed a light illuminating the heavens in the west. Slowly it grew brighter, until they could recognize it as the sun. Then everyone knew the young chief had been the victor.

All the village cheered as the canoe rounded the point, but the cheers quieted to a whisper when the people saw Big Chief was alive. The villagers rubbed their eyes in disbelief. Could this really be their old chief?

Big Chief, who had regained enough strength to talk, told the people of the heroism of Young Chief and Mouse. Big Chief then urged the wise men of the village to counsel and to decide what should be done with the sun.

The wise men deliberated for several days, discussing ways to use the sun for the benefit of people all over the world. Finally, they agreed that the sun should move about the earth, so that every village would receive light sometime during the day. This established night and day.

Young Chief Bead agreed to the decision of the wise men, and all the people of the universe praised him for his unselfishness. Although the young chief has maintained ownership of the sun even to this day, no one has challenged by proposing a contest. All the people are content with sharing the benefits of the sun.

Legend of Sway-Uock

Deep in the forest among the tallest fir trees lived an evil witch, who was known as Sway-Uock.

The very mention of her name alarmed parents and spread terror among children. She was as tall as the trees in the forest, and she could step over village houses with ease. She had a giant basket, deeper than a child was tall. Sway-Uock was greatly feared because she used the cover of darkness to slip into villages and steal children. When her giant basket was filled with screaming and crying children, she would return to her shelter and eat them for her dinner. Because of her great size, the people of the village were powerless to stop her.

Sway-Uock came out of the forest only when she was hungry. The evil witch would never bother grown-ups; children were her favorite food.

One night when Sway-Uock was very hungry, she raided a small village near the beach. As she went from house to house, she snatched boys and girls from their beds and dropped them into her huge basket. After filling her basket, the evil witch disappeared into the forest.

Sometime later, Sway-Uock made a return raid on the little village. During the second visit, many of the parents took special note of old Sway-Uock's face. Although it was dark, the fire pits threw enough light for the villagers to see her frightening features.

Her hair was matted and unkempt; her face was long and thin; and she had a crooked nose. When Sway-Uock opened her mouth, they noticed that two of her front teeth were missing.

"Those front teeth were lost when she was not careful to remove the bones," a medicine man told the people. "Her evil deeds have distorted her face and made her the ugly person she is today."

As the medicine man was talking, Sway-Uock approached the village to look for more children. The giant witch was said to have poor eyesight, but had excellent hearing. When she came to the village, Sway-Uock would creep about very quietly. Sometimes even the adults did not know she was making a raid until they heard the screams of the children in her basket.

Sway-Uock stood motionless at the edge of the forest listening for children who were making noise instead of sleeping. Every time she heard laughter or whispering, she would make a mental note of which houses contained children. When the evil witch thought she had located enough children, she went into the village and scooped them up.

During this raid Sway-Uock had a little hunchbacked boy among the children she had placed in her basket. Before starting, the witch swung the basket onto her back and secured it with braided cedar bark. While she was trudging along the trail leading through the forest, the little hunchback tried and tried to escape from the basket, but the sides were too high. He noticed that sometimes limbs of trees would brush through the basket. As one fir bough slid over Sway-Uock, part of the limb dipped low into the basket. When the limb came within reach of the little hunchback, he firmly grasped the branch and used it to swing himself out of the basket. Sway-Uock did not notice that one of her prisoners had escaped, and she continued her journey.

The boy, who was left high in the fir tree, could see very far from this vantage point. He could see the witch work her way down the hill to her house. Once home, she threw wood on her fire until the flames leaped high in the air. Then she danced around and around the fire.

Through the branches, the little hunchback could see Sway-Uock place the children on red-hot rocks at the edge of the fire. After they were cooked, the boy saw the evil witch eat every one of them.

The little hunchback could hardly believe what he had witnessed, so he was anxious to tell the people of his village. Climbing down from the fir tree, he ran home. The little boy repeated exactly what he had seen, over and over, until everyone had heard the news and all the villagers were sad.

Months later, Sway-Uock returned to the same village. During this trip, the witch filled her basket with children as she had during previous visits. But, by chance, all the children she had stolen were girls. This had never happened before, as she usually had boys in her basket as well.

As Sway-Uock lumbered along with the basket tied to her back, the girls inside worked on a plan to save themselves. "Quiet in there," the ugly witch would order. But the girls continued to plot, speaking only in low whispers.

Soon Sway-Uock arrived at her home, and after loosening the rope knots, she dropped the basket to the ground. Then the giant witch rekindled her fire and kept adding firewood until the flames leaped high. The cooking stones near the fire began to heat.

As the cooking stones got hotter and hotter, the witch decided to remove her catch from the basket and see what kind of a dinner she would have. As each girl was removed, Sway-Uock lined her up near the roaring fire. "This group will make a fine dinner," the witch said after depositing the last girl on the ground.

Sway-Uock was very pleased with her catch and began to sing and dance around the fire. "Rocks, get red hot for the little children," the witch repeated over and over as she danced.

The girls decided they would put their plan into action as the witch danced around the fire. When Sway-Uock danced by them, they planned to push her into the hot flames.

Sway-Uock had sharp hearing and overheard part of the girls' conversation. "Did I hear you say you are going to push me into the flames and destroy me?" the witch asked.

"You must have misunderstood," the little girls assured her. "We are too small to push someone as large as you into the fire." This answer satisfied Sway-Uock, and she continued to sing and dance.

When the witch danced to about the center of the row of girls, one gave the signal. As planned, they all helped topple the cruel witch into the roaring fire. When they had made sure that she was dead, the girls returned to their village.

The village was in deep mourning when the girls arrived home. Their parents were at the beach weeping, for they thought surely their children had been eaten by Sway-Uock. Laughter replaced tears when the mourners saw that the girls had survived, and they shouted triumphantly: "Sway-Uock is dead; Sway-Uock is dead!"

Happiness spread through the village, and to celebrate the occasion, the people decided to hold a great festival. Indians say this was the beginning of the potlatch celebration, where Indians get together for feasting and the giving of gifts.

The Indians found a lesson in the conquering of Sway-Uock. Despite the witch's great size, she was destroyed through the combined efforts of small girls. Working together, they were able to accomplish something that one of them working alone could never have accomplished. Women of the village proudly point out that it was girls, not boys, who were able to outsmart the cruel witch.

LEGEND OF DOH-KWI-BUHCH

The great and powerful spirit Doh-Kwi-Buhch was the creator of the world. Far to the east, he started to shape the world and placed the first people there.

When Doh-Kwi-Buhch completed forming the land in the east, he slowly moved westward. As he traveled to the west, he fashioned more of the world and of the people who were to live on it.

The Great Spirit carried a basket containing many languages, and when he created a group of people, he gave them a language. He was very careful at first to give out a language that would be the very best for the people of an area.

Doh-Kwi-Buhch eventually reached the Puget Sound country, and because he was very tired, he decided to end his task by making a great water. The West would end with the surf of these waters. Then he created tribes for the Puget Sound country and the Northland. Looking into his basket, the Great Spirit found he had many languages left. Not knowing what to do with them, he scattered the languages without regard to which people received them. That is why the Puget Sound, northern, and coastal Indians have so many different languages.

Many of the people were not happy with the way the languages were assigned. Because so many languages were in use, the different tribes could not communicate.

Few were satisfied with the way the world was created. The sky was so low, tall people would bump their heads on low clouds. Others would climb trees and make their way into the next world. The wise leaders of all the tribes knew this was not right, so they planned a great meeting.

Since different languages prevented all leaders from understanding the discussion, the leaders used sign language. They agreed that the people and creatures of the world should join to push the sky higher off the ground. The Great Spirit had given animals, birds, insects, and people different languages, so it would be difficult to tell them just when to shove. To move the sky higher, every person and creature would have to shove at the same moment.

Finally, the word "Ya-hoh" was suggested. It means "to lift together," and all the leaders agreed that this would be a fitting word to signal the start of the massive effort. All the tribes went to work making poles to lift the sky.

When the time planned for raising the sky arrived, everyone braced his pole against the sky. The great leaders gave the command "Ya-hoh," and the people lifted with all their strength. Slowly the sky was pushed higher. "Ya-hoh," came a second command, and the sky was raised a little more. With a third "Ya-hoh," the people were able to move the sky into its present position.

The raising of the sky also had an effect on the heavens. While the people were preparing to hoist the sky, three hunters were chasing four elk. The hunters had not heard that the sky was to be raised. The elk began to tire, and when they came to where the sky was very close to the earth, they leaped into the next world. Anxious for a kill, the hunters and their dog followed.

When the sky was raised, the hunters and the elk were separated from the earth. On a clear night, one can still see them in the sky. The three hunters appear as the stars forming the handle of the Dipper. One of the hunters was leading his dog, and he is the center of the handle. The faithful dog is the tiny star close to him. The four elk form the ladle part of the Dipper.

The people were proud of their part in raising the sky.

It put an end to jumping or climbing into the next world, and taught them that by working together they could accomplish much. Although they spoke different languages, they all learned a common word used when people are lifting together. "Ya-hoh" is still used by many tribes today.

VI.

Legends Told by the Makah

As remembered by the daughter of Chief Swan

The Makah Indians, a subdivision of the great Nootka people, were famous for their skill as mariners, often braving the waters of the Pacific Ocean for a month at a time in their big, pointed-prow canoes. These expeditions took them far from their home shores in quest of whales, seals, and halibut.

For centuries the Makahs have lived on the westernmost portion of the United States mainland. Their reservation is on the northwestern tip of the State of Washington with a headquarters at Neah Bay.

Helma Swan Ward, oldest surviving child of the late Chief Swan, remembers the old stories of her people as they were handed down from her great-grandfather, to her grandfather, to her father.

"My father worked hard during his life to teach and preserve the identity of our Makah culture," she recalled. "He started tribal dancing and helped revive the old dances that involved the dancer in the story told by the song." Her father's guidance gave her a rich insight into her tribal background.

"The principal occupations of the Makah Indians were

whaling, seal hunting, and fishing," Mrs. Ward said in telling how her people lived before the settlers arrived. "My grandfather was well known for his successful seal and whale hunts. When seals were killed, the skins were sold or traded, and the meat was divided among the people. A successful whale hunt meant food for an entire village."

"Sealing and whaling canoes would seat three to four men abreast and were forty to fifty feet long. One large cedar tree was used for the hull." Mrs. Ward remembered that the canoes built by her grandfather had carved bow pieces and a set of sails. Each sail had a separate design. Whalers usually carried an eleven-man crew and would stay out on the ocean for about a month.

"The men carried dried fish for food during these long trips," Mrs. Ward related. "Seal stomachs were treated and used for storing their fresh water." For warmth against chilling ocean breezes, the Makah sailors wore skins and robes, with sealskin moccasins.

Women never accompanied the men on their sea journeys. Mrs. Ward said the women of the Makah villages were busier than the women of today. They made clothes for their families, wove baskets, picked berries, and prepared foods for winter. The Makah women wore dresses they made of shredded cedar bark.

After the first white traders arrived, the Makahs accepted manufactured blankets. They often decorated them with designs bordered with rows of white pearl buttons, and wore them over their shoulders.

"My mother told me about living in the 'smokehouse' [longhouse]," she said. "It was owned and built by the community and was home for about twenty families. A group of 'smokehouses' would make up a village." Each family sharing the longhouse lived in a family section. Family sections were about the size of a barn stall.

When fishermen returned from a fishing trip, everyone in the village was notified and shared in the catch. "A fisherman would call out his success by the type of fish when he beached his canoe. Women would pass the word from family to family. It was the woman's job to go down to the beach and pick up the food her family needed from the fishermen. Catches usually included lingcod, halibut, red snapper, and black bass, which were caught on a hook and line. During the salmon runs, the fishermen would use drift nets near the mouth of the rivers."

Some of the salmon were roasted and eaten fresh, but most of this silvery harvest was smoked for winter use. Other foods were stored for use during the winter months in addition to the salmon. Huckleberries, blueberries, salal, and salmon berries were gathered and dried. The women would dig clams and slowly cook them over hot coals, smoke-drying them as a way of preparing them for storage.

Makah warriors were constantly on guard against enemy raiding parties. During such attacks, swarms of enemy war canoes would descend on the villages to loot and kidnap women. Children playing on the beach were often carried off as slaves. Historic enemies of the Makahs were Canadian Indians, Elwa, Quileute, and Taholas.

Chief Swan received his education at the Makah Reservation Boarding School just before the turn of the century. He learned the carpentry trade and worked on the reservation as a government employee for thirty-two years. Chief Swan was a skilled wood-carver and gained considerable fame for his carved pillars. Born in 1880, during his seventy-eight years he saw the canoe yield to the horse and the horse replaced by the automobile. During his life-span, he witnessed a move away from the Indian ways, and a gradual adoption of the white man's culture.

Mrs. Ward's eldest son, Arnold Hunter, is now the hereditary chief of the Makahs. The hereditary chieftainship is handed down from generation to generation to the firstborn male. In the early days, the hereditary chief governed the tribe, but now the Makahs govern themselves through an elected tribal council. These reservation councils are prescribed by federal law and function much like a city council.

ISHCUS AND THE CLAMSHELL BOY

In the early days of the Makah nation, an old woman named Ishcus roamed the hills above the coastal villages, watching them during the daylight hours. With the first signs of nightfall, Ishcus would descend from the hills and walk up and down the ocean beaches. She was easily recognized because she always had a huge basket strapped to her back. When children got close enough, she seized them and threw them into it.

Parents warned their children about Ishcus. Every youngster was cautioned to beware of strangers, to avoid anyone who carried a large basket, and always to be home well before dark.

But Ishcus was very clever at deceiving children. More

and more of them fell victim to her, and her raids became more daring. The village people made a rule that children could no longer play on the beach. They didn't want one more child lost to Ishcus.

The children loved to play on the beach and were not happy with the new restriction. At first all observed the rule, but after a few days some could no longer resist the temptation. When they thought no one was looking, they slipped out onto the white sands. None of the villagers saw the children leave, but every minute they were being watched from a nearby hill.

Ishcus knew the children would be easy prey. She hurried down the hill so that she would be able to approach them at the first sign of nightfall.

When the sun began to disappear over the ocean, Ishcus walked up the beach to where the children were still playing. "Have no fear," she called to them. "I have a nice surprise for all of you. All you have to do is come and get it."

But when the children flocked around Ishcus to receive their surprise, the old woman filled their eyes with sticky pitch. Then she dumped them into her basket and carried them deep into the hills.

When it was discovered the youngsters were missing from their homes, the parents alerted the village, and everyone rushed to the beach. There, they found marks in the sand where the children had been playing and the footprints of Ishcus leading off toward the wilderness.

"This stealing of our children must be stopped!" the chief proclaimed. "We shall send our finest warriors out to deal with this woman Ishcus."

One mother fell to her knees, overcome with grief. She cried and cried and continued to cry long after everyone had returned to their homes. Ishcus had taken her last child after stealing six others on earlier raids.

"My children, my children," the poor mother sobbed as a steady stream of tears flowed down her cheeks. She cried late into the night, until her supply of tears was almost exhausted. Then, with only one tiny tear left to trickle down her cheek, she thought about how empty her house was without her children. This thought made the last tear roll off her cheek and fall into an open clamshell on the beach.

Upon striking the shell, the tiny tear emitted a strange glow, and suddenly life began to take shape. The mother, in her great sorrow, had her face buried in her hands and did not notice what was happening.

"Why are you in such deep sorrow?" a voice asked. "Are you mourning the loss of a loved one?"

The startled woman looked around and, failing to see anyone, once again buried her face in her hands. Then the voice came again but a little stronger:

"Why are you so sad? Tell me what is troubling you."

Once again the mother looked around. At first she saw nothing, but when she glanced down, she saw a very tiny creature standing in the clamshell. Before her eyes it grew into a small boy.

"Where did you come from?" she asked. "Who are you?"

"I'm the clamshell boy. My spirit was released from this shell by your tear," he replied. "Now tell me, why have you been crying?"

"My heart is heavy because Ishcus has taken all my

children," she explained. "Not only has she carried off mine, but she has stolen nearly all of the village children."

"Cry no longer," the boy commanded. "I'll find Ishcus and return the children to their homes."

The mother warned the boy not to go after Ishcus, because she feared he too would become a victim. The boy was very handsome, and she knew that Ishcus loved to steal handsome boys.

"I'm not afraid," the boy said. "I'll search the hills for Ishcus and find the children. I shall not fail!"

Then he disappeared into the darkness.

The boy walked and walked for many days and nights, but he could not find a single clue as to where Ishcus was hiding the children. He was nearing exhaustion when he found a spring near the base of a large tree. After taking a drink of water, the boy climbed the tree and fell asleep on a large branch.

Early the next morning he was awakened by the sound of twigs cracking. Looking down, he saw Ishcus walk beneath the tree and stop at the spring for a drink of water. She got down on her knees to take a drink, and she noticed the boy's reflection in the water. Thinking it was her own, she admired it for a while, saying, "This water must contain powerful medicine. I've turned into such a handsome person with such a beautiful complexion."

Ishcus took another drink of water, washed her face, and was brushing her hair when the water cleared, and the reflection was again visible. "My, I'm handsome," she said again and again. The boy soon got tired of hearing her rave about her beauty, so he dropped a small branch into the spring.

This made Ishcus look up, and when she spotted the boy,

she said, "Oh, it was you and not me that I was admiring." The boy agreed that she had seen his reflection and not her own.

"Come down," Ishcus invited. "Tell me how you became so handsome."

The boy accepted her invitation and climbed down from the tree. He explained that every day he rubbed black rocks over his face, and the power of the rocks gave him his handsome features and complexion.

"You're such a handsome boy," Ishcus told him. "Please help me to look like you. If you will help me, I'll promise not to make you a prisoner."

They searched around the edge of the spring until they found a handful of black rocks. The ugly Ishcus took the stones and rubbed them over her face for nearly a day, but when she gazed at her reflection in the spring, she could see no improvement.

"I see no change in my appearance," said the disappointed Ishcus. "These stones contain no special power; all they did was scratch my face." She threw the black rocks to the ground and started for the boy. "I'm going to put you with the rest of the children."

"Wait," pleaded the boy. "Those stones did have power, and your face has become very pretty. You looked at your reflection in the tiny spring pool, and it distorted your lovely features. To see how really beautiful you are, we must go to a cliff high above the ocean. The ocean is much larger, and it speaks only the truth."

"Then we shall go to a cliff high above the ocean beach. If my reflection does not show great beauty, you shall pay with your life."

When they got to the cliff, Ishcus peeked over the edge

but could not see a reflection. "I see no reflection," Ishcus complained. "Is this a trick?"

"Of course you cannot see your reflection," the boy countered. "You're not leaning out far enough."

Ishcus leaned out a little farther over the edge, but complained that her image was nowhere to be seen. The boy argued she still was not leaning out far enough to see her reflection below. He promised she would clearly see her image by extending herself a little farther over the edge. When she did as he suggested, he gave her a little push and sent her hurtling to her death on the rocks far below.

With Ishcus out of the way, the boy decided to find where the children were being held captive. He walked for days. Occasionally he would climb a tree to see if any type of a dwelling was in sight.

Days later, when he had nearly decided to give up the search, the boy climbed what he thought was to be his last tree. Exhausted from the trail, he could hardly believe his eyes when he saw a small column of smoke rising from a clearing in the forest.

He was sure this was where Ishcus had lived. Following a trail through the firs, the boy came to a large house. Inside were hundreds of children hanging up to dry with pitch in their eyes. The boy took them down, removed the gum from their eyes, and returned them to their parents.

The parents celebrated the return of their children with the giving of gifts, and this is thought to be the first potlatch among the Makah people. The children learned that they must follow the laws of the tribe and be home before the sun sets.

KWATEE AND THE WOLF

In the early days, Kwatee descended from the heavens to change the earth. After making many changes, he became very hungry.

A wolf came walking down the trail, and Kwatee killed it. "Wolves are not good to eat," Kwatee thought after cooking it. "I must bury this one before the wolf pack discovers what I have done."

He had no sooner buried the wolf than he heard the pack coming down the trail. Kwatee lay by his fire and pretended he was asleep.

The wolf pack approached him. The wolf leader stepped forward and asked if Kwatee had seen their missing brother. "How could I?" Kwatee asked. "I've been asleep here by my fire all the time." The wolves left to search for their brother.

A deer wandered down the trail near Kwatee's camp, and he killed it. "This will make a fine meal," Kwatee said to himself. He ate every bit of the deer meat and made a coat of the hide.

Later the head buck and the deer tribe stopped at Kwatee's camp. "We have lost a brother," the head buck said. "Have you seen him?"

"Oh, no," answered Kwatee. "I've been right here all the time." Kwatee, sensing that the deer were suspicious, edged a little closer to the fire. When the deer were not looking, he quickly stuck his foot in the fire to singe the flesh.

The head buck noticed the coat Kwatee had made out of the hide. "It appears you might know more about our brother than you've told us," the buck said. "We think you killed our brother, ate him, and made that coat out of his hide."

"How could that happen?" Kwatee questioned. He held up his foot and showed his burns. "One must be fleet of foot to catch a deer. Does it look as though I could kill your brother with such painful burns on my foot? I can hardly walk. How could I kill him?"

"You have not explained how you got our brother's hide," the head buck said.

The wolf pack happened by again and listened to the head deer's story. "We think he has murdered our brother, too," the wolves said. "He has committed two murders!"

"See my burns," Kwatee said as he once again held his foot high so all could see.

"Those burns do not appear to be serious," the chief wolf said. "We think you are guilty."

"I have a plan for finding the true murderer," Kwatee told them. "Everyone knows about my powerful magic. We will use it to find the guilty one. He must be nearby, for he left the hide of our friends' brother right here in my camp."

The wolf pack and the deer tribe discussed Kwatee's offer. "If you can find the guilty one by using your magic, then use it. But none of your tricks," they told him. "You have tricked us many times, and we do not trust you."

"If you feel that way, put your minds at ease," Kwatee replied. "Everyone form a circle around me. I will beat the drum and sing my song of magic, and you will help find the murderer by dancing around me. Now how could I escape when you have me surrounded?"

The animals began to dance to Kwatee's song. Finally

the trickster stopped singing and asked if anyone had found the murderer. When they answered that they had seen no one but him, Kwatee advised them to widen their circle.

Once more the dancing began. After the animals had danced most of the day, Kwatee once again stopped singing and asked if anyone had captured the guilty one. Some expressed concern that the dancing was just another Kwatee trick.

"My friends," Kwatee called to the animals, "the reason my magic has not pointed out the one who has killed your brothers is because I am not dancing. You are all my friends; I shall dance with you despite my burned foot. I want to see the death of your brothers avenged."

As Kwatee took his place in the circle, he feigned pain but insisted on continuing with the dance. "We must spread out farther. We are too close together," Kwatee called to the dancers. "If we are to find the killer, there must be more space between the dancers."

The deer tribe and the wolf pack wanted to capture the killer. They followed Kwatee's suggestions and kept increasing the size of the circle until the dancers were dancing through the trees on the edge of the forest.

"We almost have the killer," Kwatee yelled. "He is close at hand. To find out who he is, we need to spread out so we have a little more room between us." This made the circle of dancers very large. Some of them were dancing far into the trees, and this is exactly what Kwatee wanted. When Kwatee danced into the forest, he slipped away undetected and never returned.

The wolf chief and the head buck powwowed after they discovered Kwatee's deception.

"This person Kwatee was sent here to teach us a lesson," the wolf chief announced. "We must tell all the animals of this deception, so they too will learn from our mistake."

"And we must remember the lesson ourselves," the head buck cautioned. "If a man deceives you once, it is your duty to take care that you aren't fooled twice."

LEGEND OF KWATEE

All the creatures in the world are as they are because Kwatee the changer decided they should be that way.

Kwatee traveled over the earth, across the mountains and up and down the beaches, changing everything. He was preparing the world for a new kind of people that were to come someday. Out of the early people Kwatee created deer, elk, and other animals.

The early people heard that Kwatee was coming long before he arrived. The news was passed on from village to village and from tribe to tribe. None of the early people wanted to be changed into new kinds of animals, or any other kind of people. So they vowed to destroy Kwatee when he arrived.

Kwatee was very shrewd. He never told anyone what he looked like or where he was going. When he visited a new area and walked into a village, the early people did not recognize him as the changer. They thought a weary traveler was going through their land, and he was never suspected.

Many moons have passed since Kwatee visited the beaches of the Washington coast. During this visit, he met a man sharpening a knife made from mussel shells.

"It looks as if you are expecting a battle," Kwatee said to the man.

"Not quite," the man replied. "I am preparing for the coming of the changer. If he starts changing things around here, I will use this knife to kill him."

"I have never seen a knife quite like that before," Kwatee told him and asked to examine it. The man handed it to him, and Kwatee carefully looked it over.

"I see you have spent many hours making a sharp point on this knife," Kwatee observed. "This should sink deep into the changer's heart and make a clean kill."

The man agreed. This was a weapon he had designed for the quick disposal of the changer.

"I too think this knife should be used," Kwatee said as he moved a step closer to the man. "It should be used to make antlers," he commanded and plunged it into the top of the man's head. "Your ears shall grow large, and you shall have two antlers protruding from your head. Your flesh shall provide food for the people who are to come, and they will call you Deer."

When Kwatee finished speaking, the newly created deer dashed off into the wilderness, which was to become his new home. After watching the deer run into the woods, Kwatee smiled his satisfaction and continued to walk the beach.

After a short walk, Kwatee found a man shaping a club. "That looks like a fine club you're making," Kwatee said as he sat down beside him. Then he asked to examine it.

"What do you plan to do with this fine club?" Kwatee asked.

"I hear a man is coming to this country who plans to

change the world. I don't want the world changed. When he arrives, I shall use that club to kill him," the man answered.

"I have a better use for it," Kwatee said and commanded the man to stand. Then Kwatee stepped behind him and pushed the small end of the club into the man's back.

"Now you shall have a tail," Kwatee told him. "You will grow a warm coat and become a fine swimmer. When the new people arrive, they will call you Beaver. Your warm coat will supply them with skins. Since you like to work with wood, you will eat bark and twigs. You will cut trees and build your house of wood. When you are frightened, you will slap your tail on the water."

When this man had completely changed into a beaver, he ran for the nearest stream, in which he would build his home. Then Kwatee continued his journey until he met a man sharpening a spear.

"Why are you making your spear so sharp?" Kwatee asked as he approached the man.

"Soon a man who is changing the world will be on this beach. When I see him, I'll use my spear to kill him," the man answered. "That will put an end to the change foolishness."

"It looks like a good spear with a sharp flint point. May I feel for myself how sharp that flint really is?" Kwatee asked. The man handed Kwatee the spear. After feeling the point, he said, "You're right. This spear will make short work of killing that changer."

Kwatee pointed the spear at the man and ordered him to turn around. He pushed the spear into him, saying, "Mink, this will be your tail. You will provide warm robes for the people to come." The sharp point of the spear helped form mink's teeth, and that is why mink have such sharp teeth.

Near Neah Bay, Kwatee noticed many fierce dogs but saw no people. This country is too beautiful to be without people, Kwatee thought, and he caught a male and a female dog. He changed them into people. Then he changed all the other wild dogs into people.

"These people will make fine fishermen," Kwatee said. He taught them to build long canoes and to hunt the whale. They learned to fish for halibut and hunt deer.

The new people were fierce warriors, and many eventually spread out to find new lands to conquer. Those who settled in villages near Lake Ozette and Neah Bay grew very fast. That is why the modern Makahs are big people.

VII.

Legends of the Canoe Indians

As told by Chief Martin Sampson

Swinomish Chief Martin Sampson was considered dean of Pacific Northwest Indian storytellers until his death in 1980.

Born the day before Independence Day in the year 1888, Chief Sampson's memory dated back to the infancy of Washington's statehood and to firsthand accounts of his people's early culture. As a youth, he was fascinated with legends he learned from his grandmother, Pautchtowlo, who was the historian for her band. He credited these and legends told by his mother with making the greatest impression on his childhood.

Indian education for Martin Sampson was no different from that of other reservation youngsters of that time. His mother's and grandmother's stories taught him tribal history, Indian religion, mixing of herbs for the infirm, and the use of medicine powers. He learned to preserve salmon and between salmon runs young Sampson was taught the logging trade before he started formal classroom schooling.

Both his grandmother and mother were medicine squaws who performed Indian cures. Chief Sampson's grandmother produced medicine reported to be so powerful that she could heal a severe headache by reciting three sacred words and gently blowing on the cranium of the stricken person.

Chief Sampson explains that medicine powers have been a part of his family's heritage for centuries.

Stories telling of the medicine used by Chief Sampson's forebears date back to before the first white settler set foot in the Puget Sound country. One such anecdote tells of a vision one of his ancestors had. The man's name was Lacailaby. The vision revealed that an epidemic was coming and warned the people to retire to their longhouse near La Conner, Washington.

The people obeyed the wisdom of the vision, and they remained in their longhouse, singing and dancing, for many days. This saved their lives, for in this way they avoided exposure to smallpox. The deadly disease, introduced by the crew of an explorer's ship, swept through village after village, killing many people.

Before the smallpox epidemic struck, Indians estimate the Swinomish tribe had more than a thousand people. Only 250 persons survived that epidemic, and today the tribe has about four hundred members on its rolls.

In 1890, when Chief Sampson was two years old, a second smallpox epidemic struck the Swinomish Indians. He recalls stories about people burning their houses and belongings to kill the dreaded disease. Although it took many lives, a higher percentage survived than did during the first epidemic.

Formal education for Martin Sampson started at the Chemawa Indian School near Salem, Oregon. A special scholarship award sent him on to Hampton College in Virginia, where he became the first Washington Indian to receive a college degree. Sampson's diploma is a part of the Indian collection on display at Skagit County Historical Society Museum in Mount Vernon, Washington.

Born the son of hereditary Swinomish Chief Joseph Sampson, earlier known as Joseph Sam, Martin Sampson was named to be a Swinomish chief by a retiring uncle in 1930. More than five hundred fellow tribesmen and Indians visiting from nearby reservations attended the ceremonies. At that time, he accepted responsibility for maintaining the tribal traditions, legends, and language as well as representing his people on all treaty matters with the United States government.

When the United States entered World War I, American Indians were not citizens and were not entitled to the privileges that accompanied citizenship, yet they were intensely patriotic. Although he was twenty-nine years of age, Sampson was one of six Swinomish who rallied to the cause.

He was honorably discharged from the army on December 31, 1918, at Vancouver Barracks, Washington. At that moment he became a citizen of the United States, and it was one of his proudest moments. An Act of Congress granted all Indians full citizenship in 1924, some six years later.

Martin Sampson started his civil-service career in 1913, and before retiring in 1958 at seventy years of age, he had seen service at Indian reservations and facilities in Oregon, Montana, and Washington. After retiring he taught his native Salish language at the University of Washington and at one time was employed as a television weatherman under the name Chief Morning Cloud.

The Swinomish Indians were a canoe tribe living near the mouth of the Skagit River. Their tribal occupations included fishermen, hunters, warriors, and wood-carvers or canoe makers. Today, they share a reservation near La Conner, Washington, with Samish and Skagit Indians.

Chief Sampson's mother, known as Gwakotsa among the Indians and as Susie Peters by the white settlers, noticed a change in her people over the years. She was born in 1866 and died in 1961 at the age of ninety-five years.

Chief Sampson recalls his mother's words regarding the change in her people. She told him, "When I was a young woman, speaking in our own language, we always referred to friends and relatives as 'my esteemed friend' or 'my revered cousin.' Nowadays, the only thing they can say is 'my poor friend' or 'poor person.'"

Children of the early Swinomish would amuse themselves by playing games or imitating their elders. One contest popular among the boys was competing with bow and arrow. The contestants would shoot for distance, with the longest shot claiming all the arrows. Tug-of-war, using a long pole instead of a rope, was played by both boys and girls. Many copied the songs and actions of the medicine man in treating a patient.

Medicine men would sing their own special songs while working on a patient. Chief Sampson's uncle, Jim Mc-Cloud, was famous for his healing powers. Here is a translation of his medicine man's song:

> Into a spirit canoe . . . it sails to the land of the Spirits.
> In the middle of the river is a Spirit House.
> When Jimmy McCloud enters, the canoe shouts, "I have
>   brought you a human."

The Spirits showed him great wealth and promised, "You will receive all of this if you help people."

Then the Spirits took him to the other end of the house.

There were skeletons and bones of people who had been conquered and destroyed.

The Spirits then said, "Either can be yours, it's up to you."

Songs like the one that gave Jim McCloud his medicine power usually came to the owner when he was quite young. Chief Sampson's mother received her song of medicine when she was ten years of age.

The legends held a special meaning for his mother. "They helped her to take life as it came; nothing seemed to depress her, and she was always optimistic," he recalled. "The old stories provided strength and values for all of us."

Today the legends of the Canoe Indians are slowly passing with the old-timers who told them. But the stories that remain still provide a valuable explanation of the past for all who are willing to listen.

THE FIRST QUEDELISH

Early Indians, hoping to become medicine doctors, would seek power through fasting and watching for a sign from the spiritual world.

Sometimes when young Skagit River Indians aspired to become medicine men, they would hike to the shores of Big Lake in what is now Skagit County, Washington. Once there, they'd fast until the Great Spirit spoke.

It was during such a fast that a young man heard a voice come from beneath the lake's surface. The voice told him that if he was to become a doctor, he must enter the spirit world.

"Build a raft and go to the center of the lake," the voice instructed. "Then dive to the bottom, where you will find great power."

The young man knew the lake was very deep at the point where he was to enter the water. After building a raft, he found a large boulder and securely attached twelve feet of cedar-bark rope to it. Then he placed it on the raft and paddled to a point near the center of the lake.

As the raft approached where he was to enter the water, the young man called to the spirit voice: "How will I find breath beneath these waters?"

"You must have faith that we will allow no harm to come to you," the spirit replied. "Do not fish swim deep below the lake's surface and yet survive?"

The young man wrapped the loose end of the cedar rope two turns around his right wrist and then kicked the huge boulder attached to the other end into the water. The heavy rock pulled him beneath the surface and into the depths of the lake.

At the bottom he was greeted by two men. They took him to an underwater longhouse, where many people were waiting.

"We wish to honor you," a chief told him. "You have been selected to take an important message to all the people of your world. But first, we shall have a great feast and celebration."

The young man ate and danced with his underwater friends for three days. When the time came for him to return to his people, a beautiful maiden dressed in white buckskin handed him two cedar disks. "Take these and learn of their value," she told him. The maiden then turned into a large salmon and swam away.

The two men who had first greeted him took the young man by the arm and started to swim to the lake's surface. "You've much to learn before we surface, so listen very carefully," they told him.

"You must tell everyone in the world about the cedar disks that were given to you," the men said. "They represent twin brothers whom you will know as 'clean mind' and 'clean body.' If these brothers are kept together, they become powerful guides. The brothers will guide fish to the net of the fisherman, provide game for the arrow of the hunter, and will grant safekeeping to the warrior who goes into battle."

The young man promised to remember these words so that he could relay them to the world. He assured his underwater companions that he'd always wear the disks, called Quedelish by the Indians.

When the young man awakened from what seemed to be a deep sleep, he was sprawled out on the deck of his raft. Clutched in each hand was a cedar disk, reminding him that what he had experienced was much more than a dream.

True to his word, the young man traveled across the land telling the story of the Quedelish. From the Puget Sound country he crossed the mountains and covered the lands to the east. Each tribe he visited learned of the Quedelish, and they told others of its meaning.

Indians make the Quedelish from cedar or soft wood,

vine maple, and sometimes buckskin. When these disks were used to decorate a necklace or feather bonnet, they offered the power of the twin brothers to the wearer. To be worthy of this sign, the Indians bathed frequently and offered daily prayers to purify their minds.

The word of the Quedelish spread to most tribes of North America. It is still used on war bonnets and special head-dresses, and many modern Indians wear a pair of disks on a necklace.

Universal Story of the Sasquatch

In the early days of mankind, a warlike band of northern Indians would raid the peaceful villages of the south to kill, plunder, and take slaves.

The southern coastal villages would maintain lookouts to provide a warning if northern war canoes approached. The lookouts had to be on guard constantly, for no one could predict when an attack might take place.

One morning, a fleet of northern war canoes was sighted heading toward the village. The great chief called the society of warriors and outlined a plan to ambush the raiders.

When the northerners beached their canoes, a village maiden was sent to attract their attention and then to decoy them into a brush-filled gully. Defenders were concealed in the gully, and they attacked from all sides as the last group of northerners entered the trap.

Not one invader survived the battle, and many bodies covered the ground. After the skirmish, the chief called the people to a village meeting.

"My people, you must not touch the bodies of the enemy

dead. They contain evil spirits," the chief called out. "These evil spirits will be leaving the dead and looking for the living. Only the medicine men can handle their burial." He then ordered the tribal medicine men to bury the dead by placing their bodies on racks placed high in the trees.

Sometime later, a medicine man was sent to examine these burial racks. He was surprised to find the enemy bodies were missing, although the racks were still well secured to the trees. The medicine man hurried back to the village to counsel with the other shamans of his tribe.

"My brothers, I'm very concerned," he told the medicine council. "Something very strange has happened to the enemy bodies. They have vanished, and yet the burial racks are secure and show no evidence of animal damage."

One aged medicine man, known for his great wisdom, was asked what had happened. "This is the work of the spirits," he explained. "Some spirit other than human has claimed these bodies."

As time passed, sightings of giant, animallike people were reported. The tribal medicine council agreed that these creatures were formed when animal spirits entered the bodies of evil warriors. Over the years, the bodies of many warriors who were slain in battle disappeared from their burial racks. Every time the body of an evil person was hung on a rack, it would disappear. Then a large, hairy, animal-like person would be seen near the burial tree.

The Indians noticed that these creatures had a great fear of being seen. To avoid people, they traveled many miles through the wilderness. Indians from British Columbia to California reported sighting this human-shaped animal. Because these animals fled in panic when a human was sighted, many of the Indian tribes called them Kauget, which means "one who runs and hides." Other tribes, speaking a different language, used the word "Sasquatch" to describe them.

On one occasion, an Indian recognized the facial features of a Sasquatch as those of a recently deceased tribal member. He called out the name of his late friend, and the Sasquatch went wild with fear. The large creature was reported to have crashed into the dense forest, leaving a trail of shattered and fallen trees in his wake. The Indians agree that the sound of his human name holds one of the Sasquatch's greatest fears.

These animal people never stop growing. They are powerful and can easily swim the largest rivers. Some can lift huge boulders with little effort, while others have been known to uproot the largest trees to show off their strength.

Even to this day, the Sasquatch continue to exist. Occasionally white men have reported seeing a huge manlike monster in this region, and some scientists take such reports seriously. The Sasquatch have never been known to attack the living, but Indians warn that because the Sasquatch were resurrected from bodies of fierce warriors and evil persons, they could be very dangerous.

RAVEN AND THE PHEASANT

Raven and Pheasant were the high magistrates of their day. For all the creatures of the world, the word of this pair was law.

One afternoon Raven decided to demonstrate his hunting prowess by slaying an elk with a single arrow. He took some of his followers along to witness his feat. One spotted a bull elk and pointed it out to Raven.

"That elk is far out of range for your bow, we'll have to stalk him," he said.

"For your bow maybe, but not for mine," Raven snapped back. Sighting down the shaft, Raven drew back on the bowstring and let the arrow fly. It went straight to its mark and dropped the big bull.

"Let that be a lesson to all of you," Raven told those assembled. "My marksmanship with the arrow is a symbol of my great power. You must remember I'm your magistrate!"

When Raven approached his kill, he found that a stranger was standing beside the dead animal. "I'm the changer, who was sent to this country by the Great Spirit," he said. "Now tell me, who owns that elk?"

"Did you not see my great shot?" Raven asked. "I killed the elk, and he's mine."

"My friend, you're wrong," Changer answered. "That elk is mine."

"Don't you know whom you are challenging?" Raven questioned. "I'm the magistrate, and if I say I killed this elk, then he belongs to me, and you have no argument."

"All right, then, who owns that dog sitting at your feet?" Changer inquired.

"It's my dog," replied Raven. "The dog belongs to me and no one else!"

"We must disagree once more, my friend," Changer stated. "I also own that animal."

"Impossible," declared Raven. "I raised that dog from a tiny puppy. You had nothing to do with it."

"Let's determine the owner of this dog by a simple contest. We'll both call the animal, and he'll point out the true owner by obeying his call. Since you're a high magistrate and believe in fairness, you should find this proposal most acceptable."

Raven agreed to the terms of the proposition and started to call the dog. When the animal ignored him, Raven became furious and ran to it. Instead of acting as though Raven were his master, the dog snarled and attacked.

"You've had your opportunity," Changer said. "Now I shall try." Then Changer called it by name, saying, "Come, Tobalish, come, Tobalish." It responded by running to Changer's side, wagging its tail as any dog does when called by its master.

"See there, that's my dog," Changer stated. "And that is my elk as well."

"But I don't understand," Raven said. "How can these be yours?"

"The Great Spirit owns all the creatures of the universe, and they are here for you to use, not to own," Changer answered. "Now take the dog and enjoy his companionship. He's for you to use, as is the elk."

"How do I know that what you say is true?" inquired Raven.

"If you still doubt that what has happened here today is evidence of the wisdom of my words, then when you arrive at your shelter you will receive an unmistakable sign," Changer replied.

Raven related the story of his elk hunt to his wife when

he arrived home, and when they went out to look at the elk, it had turned into a rotten log.

It so happened that Pheasant went elk hunting that same afternoon. Like Raven, he, too, made a fine shot and killed a large bull elk. As Pheasant approached his kill, he found Changer standing beside the animal.

"Tell me, my friend, who owns this fine bull elk?" Changer asked.

"It would seem it was yours, lent to me by my master," Pheasant replied.

"Take the elk home, Pheasant, and hold a feast for your family," Changer commanded.

A few years later when Pheasant and Raven were making the rules of the universe, Pheasant's son died. Pheasant called on Raven to suggest legislation for longer life.

"My son died right at the beginning of his manhood, and I don't think that is right. I believe we should grant every young person the right to a full life."

"Don't be foolish," Raven replied. "The death of your son has affected your judgment. Let the young die and let the old die. If everyone lived, our food supply would soon be gone. Do you want to be responsible for starting a famine?"

"All right, my neighbor," Pheasant responded. "Although I miss my son very much, I'll abide by your wisdom."

A few weeks later, Raven's son died. He rushed to Pheasant saying, "We must change the law and allow our young men to live full lives. If we don't, I fear we will have a great shortage of mature thinking."

"Maybe you're right," Pheasant replied, "but I came to

you with the same proposition when my son died, and you said, 'Let the young die and let the old die.' I agreed with you then, and we made the law. Now it cannot be changed."

LEGEND OF THE SASQUATCH

"Sasquatch" is the popular name for the humanlike monster said to inhabit the rugged mountain areas from British Columbia to California. The Skagit River Indian bands called these creatures See-Atco and explain their origin with this story.

Sometime in the dim past, a warring band from the Nookachamis tribe swept down from the hills and attacked the Utsaladdy Indians. The fierce Nookachamis warriors killed many of the Utsaladdy and forced the survivors to abandon their village.

To escape death, the terror-stricken Utsaladdy climbed into their canoes and paddled across Skagit Bay to the safety of Whidbey Island. They settled on the beach between what is now Oak Harbor and Coupeville, Washington.

Joining with a smaller band of Skagits who inhabited that area, the refugees developed a mysterious form of self-hypnotism that gave them the ability to see in the dark. During the daylight hours, they learned to cast a spell on themselves so that they became invisible to all who were not members of their band.

By studying and perfecting this secret hypnotic practice, they slowly evolved into a different people. Their appearance became almost apelike, and they grew to be the size of giants. But they were not hostile people because they retained the peaceful disposition of the Utsaladdy.

Because they had been attacked by raiding war parties so often, and because they were ashamed of their animal-like features, the people would run and hide if they saw a stranger. Sometimes they became so frightened of an approaching visitor that they would make themselves invisible for days.

An example of this ability to disappear was demonstrated just after the first white settlers arrived on Whidbey Island.

A group of men were cutting timber when they ran across a See-Atco woman. Maneuvering between the woman and the timber, they managed to block her escape route.

Three or four of the men closed in until they were almost within arms' reach. The men had agreed to seize the creature, on a prearranged signal, and take her back to show their townsfolk. When the signal was sounded, the men rushed toward the apelike woman, but they ended up holding onto each other. The elusive See-Atco had vanished.

To avoid any further interference from the white settlers, the See-Atco left the island and settled in the most remote areas of the Cascade Mountains. Deep in the heavily forested areas miles from any settlement, there have been occasional sightings reported by both Indians and whites.

In more recent times, the Indians say the See-Atco have developed even greater size and strength. With each passing decade, their bodies become more animal-like and covered with longer hair. Through their ancient practice of self-hypnotism, they are said to be so powerful that larger See-Atco can easily uproot the tallest of trees. This is an impossible task for even the finest team of horses.

For those who plan to visit See-Atco country, the old Indians advise against molesting them. Although they usually follow their peaceful Utsaladdy heritage, one never knows what a See-Atco might do.